SCAPA FLOW

in

War and Peace

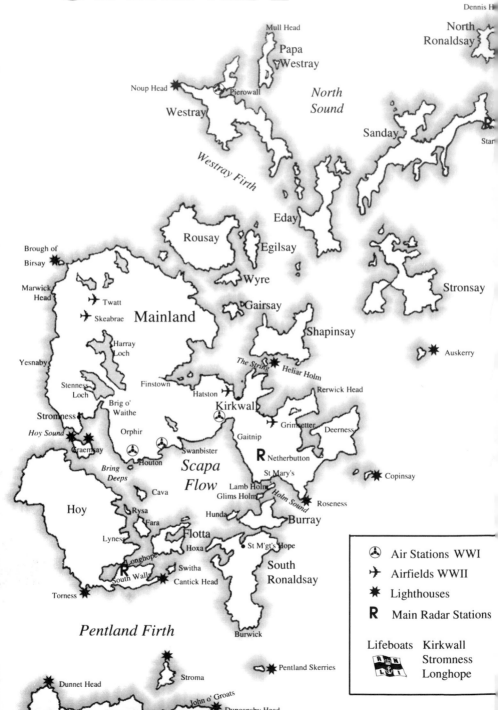

ORKNEY

Dennis H

North
Ronaldsay

Mull Head

Papa
Westray

Noup Head
Pierowall

North
Sound

Sanday

Star

Westray

R

Westray Firth

Eday

Brough of
Birsay

Rousay

Egilsay

Marwick
Head

Wyre

Stronsay

Twatt

Gairsay

Skeabrae   Mainland

Harray
Loch

Shapinsay

Yesnaby

The String   Heliar Holm   Auskerry

Finstown

Stenness
Loch

Hatston

Rerwick Head

Brig o'
Waithe

Kirkwall

Stromness

Grimsetter   Deerness

Hoy Sound

Orphir

Gaitnip

Graemsay

Swanbister

R Netherbutton

Bring
Deeps

Houton

Scapa
Flow

St Mary's

Copinsay

Cava

Lamb Holm
Glims Holm

Roseness

Hoy

Rysa

Hunda

Fara

Burray

Lyness

Flotta

Longhope

Hoxa

St M'gt's Hope

Swintha

South
Ronaldsay

South Wall

Cantick Head

Torness

Burwick

Pentland Firth

Pentland Skerries

Dunnet Head

Stroma

John o' Groats

Duncansby Head

⚓ Air Stations WWI	
✈ Airfields WWII	
✴ Lighthouses	
R Main Radar Stations	

Lifeboats Kirkwall
           Stromness
           Longhope

SCAPA FLOW

in

War and Peace

W. S. Hewison

1995
Bellavista Publications

ISBN 0 9525350 0 9

Second Edition 1996 (Reprinted)

Printed by the Kirkwall Press, Victoria Street, Kirkwall, Orkney.

Published by Bellavista Publications, Bellavista, Carness Road, Kirkwall, Orkney, KW15 1TB. Tel. 01856 872306.

Dedication

To

*They that go down to the sea in ships; and occupy
their business in great waters . . .*

The author has donated his royalties to the
Royal National Lifeboat Institution

Registered Charity No. 209603

Preface

Old soldiers never die, we are told, but they certainly fade away taking their memories with them. As a result at least two generations have grown up in Orkney, who can have no first-hand recollection of what happened in and around Scapa Flow during the second World War, and hardly anyone to remember the first. After all it is half a century since the guns fell silent giving these younger generations the chance of growing up in some sort of peace and freedom from fear. In many ways they are fortunate in never having to endure the privations and dangers that came from living around Britain's most prestigious naval base when Scapa was the strategic hub of Britain's wartime naval endeavour.

Looking across its placid waters today, however, it is difficult for them, and Orkney's many visitors, to realise that some of the most momentous events in modern history either happened in or were initiated, from this sheltered anchorage - but they did and it is the object of this book to record as concisely as possible some of those events and what led up to them, the visiting statesmen and the military leaders who controlled these events and most of all the fortitude of the servicemen and women who kept watch and ward for all those long years.

Anyone writing about Scapa Flow must inevitably rely heavily on other people's memories of what actually happened there during the wars. And quite often such information comes from casual conversations with ex-servicemen who had served at Scapa and, especially with local families and friends who had lived in the islands right through the war. Most of them probably never realised that besides having a friendly chat they were passing on such valuable information and to all of them, too numerous to name, I tender my heart-felt thanks.

Among the more formal sources of information pride of place must go to Bobby Leslie, Orkney's Chief Librarian and his staff which, of course, includes the County Archivist, Alison Fraser and the Photographic Archivist, David Mackie, whose friendly and informed assistance like that of the County Museums Officer, Bryce Wilson, never fails.

I must also express my gratitude to Mr Jim Miller, proprietor of 'The Orcadian' and his staff for all their help and for affording me such ready access to their invaluable files.

Further afield I am deeply indebted to the staff of the Imperial War Museum, especially Mr John Delaney of the Department of Photographs and also to the staff of the Public Records Office at Kew for their help and courteous cooperation.

Finally I would like to thank my publisher, Stewart Davidson, with his detailed knowledge of the printing trade for his expert advice and for keeping me to my deadlines, and my long-suffering wife, Nancy, who in spite of having had Scapa sluicing through her sitting room for the second time in ten years has shown such forbearance as to play a very active part in the layout and design of the book as well as undertaking the chore of proof-reading which she shared with Stewart's wife, Leslie.

W. S. H.

Kirkwall, 1995

Contents

Facts, Figures And Points Of View

Foreword

by

Brigadier S. P. Robertson, MBE, TD, DL

LIFE VICE PRESIDENT OF THE RNLI

I have known Bill Hewison for over sixty years, and therefore we are very old friends. Flattery however has never entered into our relationship and what I write therefore is a true assessment of this book, skilfully condensed from his detailed history 'This Great Harbour Scapa Flow'.

The position of Scapa Flow, encapsulated as it is by our South Isles, has ensured that Orkney over the centuries has played an infinitely more important part than if the islands had been merely a small group without this magnificent sheltered harbour. Peripheral though our situation is today, it was central in the days of our Norse ancestors and during the two World Wars.

Adding greatly to the appreciation of our history, this book tells a dramatic and exciting story unfolding over the centuries from Viking days and before, until the coming of today's nuclear powered warships. Looking over the sparkling blue waters of the Flow on a summer's day with the heather-clad hills of Hoy in the background, it is easy to forget that the seabed must be whitened with the bones of men who lost their lives in its waters over the ages, some because of major disasters in the 1914-18 War, and in the Second World War as related in these pages. So too have many of our crofter/fishermen in their small lobster boats met disaster underneath the beetling cliffs below which they set their creels.

In Orkney every year brings a crop of new books. This particular volume, however, is special in that it is the first to be published by Bellavista Publications, the owner being of Papa Westray extraction, and the name being that of a ship which was wrecked off the Mull Head there about fifty years ago. The well established author's family have Westray connections going back historically to the wreck of a ship from the Spanish Armada on that island.

I must not forget the part that Nancy, Bill's wife, has played in the production of this book, for I know the most intensive effort has been made by both of them to ensure that we now have this gem, which will give so much pleasure and information to our many visitors and Orcadians alike.

It is with the greatest enthusiasm that I commend it not only for this reason, but also because very generously all the royalties are to go to the Royal National Lifeboat Institution.

Sidney Robertson

Daisybank
Kirkwall
Orkney

The Great Harbour

. . . Far off the silent, changing sound was still,
   With the black islands lying thick around.

He saw each separate height, each vaguer hue,
   Where the massed islands rolled in mist away,
And though all ran together in his view
   He knew that unseen straits between them lay.

                    EDWIN MUIR
                    "Childhood"

Scapa Flow

Scapa Flow, the Royal Navy's main United Kingdom strategic base and harbour in two World Wars, has played a vital role in British maritime history for over two hundred years. From 1914 to 1918 during the first war Britain's Grand Fleet was anchored in it poised ready to deny the North Sea and Atlantic Ocean to Germany's battle fleet and merchant ships; again from 1939 to 1945 the Home Fleet used it for the same purpose to contain Hitler's navy in World War II. Even earlier, during the Napoleonic Wars of 1789-1815, it had been used as a rendezvous base for merchantmen awaiting naval escort to the Baltic.

But the strategic value of this large landlocked harbour enclosed by the South Isles of Orkney lying off the north coast of Scotland with easy access to the North Sea and the Atlantic Ocean has been recognised by mariners throughout history.

The Vikings, for instance, knew and used Scapa Flow as a raiding base as early as the 7th century AD even before they colonised the islands and it was they who named it. 'Scapa' comes from the Old Norse words, *'skalpr'* meaning *sword scabbard* but which could also be used poetically for *ship*, and *'ei'* an *isthmus* so giving *'skalpei'*, a *ship isthmus*, in other words, a place like Scapa Bay on the narrow neck of land just south of Kirkwall where they could beach their galleys on a sandy shore. 'Flow' comes from O.N. *'floi'* or *'fljot'* meaning plenty of water or a fjord, so *'skalpei floi'* - a place with plenty of water where ships could be hauled.

However, long before those Norse marauders first

sailed their longships into the Flow it had been well
known to prehistoric men of the Stone, Bronze and Iron
Ages and, of course, the Picts. There is ample evidence that
all of them lived around the Flow at one time or another
leaving behind them such archaeological reminders as the
Tomb of the Eagles in South Ronaldsay, the mysterious
Dwarfie Stone among the hills in Hoy or the various
brochs which guarded the shores, possibly against Roman
slave-raiders, before the Norsemen came. It is, however,
only from the times when these Vikings first raided and
then settled in Orkney that there is any written record of
what was happening in and around the Flow. Indeed
much of what is known of this six-century-long period of
Norse occupation comes from their sagas, especially the
Orkneyinga Saga, the history of the Orkney Earls handed
down orally from generation to generation until it was
finally committed to writing in Iceland during the 13th
century.

The Early Story

There is a place lies North where Germany
Is bounded, where stands in the rigid sea
Thule, to which there do lie opposite,
Infamous rocks, the Mariners that fright,
And a huge stony gulf, which fiercely knocks
The roaring waves against the ragged rocks;
These, if we may give credit unto fame,
Were called *Orcades* from a Greek name.

CLAUDIUS CLAUDIANUS (C. 400 AD),
Tr. by JAMES WALLACE

In Viking Times

One early and important saga date for the Flow is 995 AD when Earl Sigurd the Stout of Orkney was 'converted' to Christianity by King Olaf Trygvasson of Norway, who was returning to secure his kingdom after a foray in the West during which he had himself been converted, and forsaking the old Norse gods, had become an extremely enthusiastic Christian. Sailing east through the Pentland Firth on his way home he surprised and captured Sigurd who was anchored in Osmundswall (now Kirk Hope) near Longhope at the southern entrance to the Flow and offered him and his followers the choice between conversion to Christianity or death. Sigurd pragmatically chose conversion but seems to have reverted to the old religion before his death on Good Friday 1014 at the Battle of Clontarf outside Dublin, wrapped in the magic raven banner of the ancient faith woven by his 'wise-woman' mother, Edna, which brought victory to all who followed it but death to anyone who carried it.

Celtic missionaries had, in fact, brought Christianity to Orkney in Pictish times long before the Norsemen came.

Appreciating the strategic value of the Flow as a secure base from which their war-galleys could raid the coasts of Britain, Ireland and even into the Mediterranean, the Norsemen augmented its natural defences with castles at two of the main entrances - Paplay covering Holm Sound on the east and Cairston near Stromness overlooking Hoy Sound in the west. Between these the earls had one of their main great houses at the Bu in Orphir on the shores of the Flow itself, where Earl Haakon built the Round Church on the model of the Church of the Holy Sepulchre in Jerusalem, which he had seen during a pilgrimage to Rome and the Holy Land to receive absolution for the murder of his cousin and joint-ruler of Orkney, Magnus, in 1117. Magnus was later canonised becoming Orkney's patron saint to whom the Kirkwall Cathedral is dedicated. Only the apse of the Round Church still remains above ground today.

Another key date in the Sagas is 1263 when King Haakon Haakonson of Norway gathered his fleet of over a hundred war-galleys, the greatest assemblage of fighting ships ever seen until then, in Orkney waters. It was a show of force to re-assert his dwindling authority over the Norse possessions in Scotland but he had left it too late. An elderly man - he was called Haakon the Old - he had delayed setting out from Norway until late in the year. Summer was nearly over when he eventually sailed out through Hoxa Sound from Ronaldsvoe (now St Margaret's Hope) into the Pentland Firth and down through the Western Isles to the Clyde coast for the indecisive Battle of Largs where the real victors were the early autumn gales. With the onset of winter the storm-shattered remnants of his fleet limped back to lick its wounds in the sanctuary of the Flow. Haakon himself died that Yuletide in the Bishops' Palace close by St Magnus Cathedral where he was buried until spring when his body was taken to Scapa and put on board a ship for its last Voar cruise to Bergen in Norway and final interment with his ancestors.

The Scots Take Over

Iff ye will lye in Orkney cast anker south
or southwest from Kirkwall in the sound and
ye sall find x or xij fadomes.

ALEXANDER LINDSAY
A Rutter of the Scottish Seas c. 1540

Islands In Pawn

The 16th century saw a number of important happenings in the Flow, as for instance in 1529 when the Sinclair Earl of Caithness and his force sailed across it ostensibly to put down an island rebellion against the royal authority of James V of Scotland, but also to settle some internal Sinclair family scores. The islands had come under Scottish rule only 61 years before in 1468 when King Christian I of Denmark pledged his possessions in them as part payment of his daughter Margaret's dowry on her marriage to James III of Scotland. The pledge was not redeemed and in 1471 Orkney was annexed by the Scottish Crown. The islanders, however, did not always see eye-to-eye with their new rulers.

The two forces met on the Mainland at Summerdale under the Orphir hills in the last land-battle to be fought on Orkney soil and Caithness lost, the Earl being among the slain. Some legends claim that the Orkneymen won through divine intervention when their patron saint, Magnus, appeared on the battlefield urging them on to victory - others suggest that witchcraft played a part. At all events the Caithness men were well and truly routed.

Eleven years later in 1540 James V himself, accompanied by his powerful aide, Cardinal Beaton, Primate of Scotland, came to Orkney with several thousand men in a fleet of 16 ships and anchored in the Flow - probably in Scapa Bay - during their voyage round Scotland to keep the clan chieftains of the Highlands and Western Isles in order. They were entertained in Kirkwall by the Bishop of Orkney, Robert Maxwell and on board his

flagship, the *Salamander,* James had as pilot, Alexander
Lindsay who had compiled the 'Rutter of the Scottish
Seas', sailing instructions for mariners, describing in
considerable detail the hazards of tide, weather and coastal
features they might encounter in these waters. The
Pentland Firth and entrances to the Flow get special
mention and Lindsay's warnings hold good to this day as
the Royal Navy found out, sometimes to its cost, in the two
World Wars.

The Elizabethan mariner, Sir Martin Frobisher, seems
to have stopped off in the Flow for water and provisions in
1576 during his voyage to North America in search of the
elusive North West Passage to the Orient. But, surprisingly,
there is no record of any of the Spanish Armada galleons
having sought shelter in it from the gales which drove
them round the north of Scotland in 1588 although legend
has it that one was wrecked near Yesnaby on the west
coast of the Mainland and another, the *El Gran Grifon,*
certainly came to grief further north on Fair Isle between
Orkney and Shetland.

In 1650 the Marquis of Montrose embarked his troops,
many of them Orcadians, at St Mary's, Holm on the east
side of the Flow, for the disastrous battle of Carbisdale in
Sutherland where his Royalist cause foundered and he was
eventually taken prisoner and hanged in Edinburgh.

Orkney in general was not deeply involved in the
Jacobite rebellions of the 18th century although quite a few

of the lairds supported the Stuart cause and during the 1745 Rising a small force of Highlanders did land in Walls to collect funds for their campaign. They crossed the Flow to Kirkwall which they occupied for a time and then withdrew. A Government warship was in Stromness at the time but the two forces did not meet. After the battle of Culloden in 1746 a number of the Jacobite lairds in Orkney were hunted by Government troops, their estates confiscated and their houses burned down.

Also during the 18th century the Caithness-born but Orkney-reared John Gow, the eponymous 'Pirate' of Sir Walter Scott's novel, dropped anchor off Stromness, where he had spent his youth, and in 1725 he sacked the Hall of Clestrain on the Orphir shore. Captured after his ship grounded on the Calf of Eday in the North Isles he was taken to London for trial and ended up in Execution Dock at Wapping on the Thames.

John Rae, (1813-1893) celebrated Arctic explorer was born and brought up at the same Hall of Clestrain. His father was agent for the Hudson's Bay Company which from 1702 right into the mid-20th century recruited Orcadians for service in the far north of Canada. Until 1891 the company's ships called at Stromness in June each year to take on men, supplies and water. At one time three-quarters of the company's employees were Orcadians.

During the 19th and early 20th centuries there was a thriving fishing industry round the Flow with Stromness,

Holm, Burray and St Margaret's Hope very busy ports
during the summer herring fishing with hundreds of boats
working out of them. The introduction of steam trawlers
which could take their catches direct to markets further
south killed off the Orkney fisheries to a great extent,
although in the North Isles the Stronsay fishing lasted well
into the 1920s. The sinking of blockships in World War I
across the eastern channels into the Flow also had an
adverse affect on local herring fisheries and the building of
the Churchill Barriers across the sounds in World War II
finished them off.

The Naval Era Begins

. . . the art of Man, aided by all the Dykes, Sea Walls or Break-Waters that could possibly be built could not have contained a better Roadstead than the peculiar situation and extent of the South Isles of Orkney have made Scapa Flow . . . from whatever point the Wind blows a Vessel in Scapa Flow may make a fair wind of it out to free sea . . . a property which no other Roadstead I know of possesses, and without waiting for Tide on which account it may be called the Key to both Oceans.

GRAEME SPENCE,
Maritime Surveyor to the Admiralty, 1812

A Northern Base

The story of Scapa Flow as a Royal Navy base really begins in 1812 when an Orcadian, Graeme Spence, one-time Maritime Surveyor to the Admiralty, basing his suggestions on charts prepared by his uncle, the cartographer Murdo Mackenzie in 1750, recommended it to their Lordships as a 'Rendezvous Base' pointing out that with its numerous entrances and adequate depth it could be used by men o' war at virtually any state of wind or tide.

During the Napoleonic Wars Longhope, near the southern entrances with its long fjord-like bay and proximity to the Pentland Firth, was used as a marshalling harbour for Baltic-bound merchant ships waiting for a naval escort to see them safely across the North Sea, the English Channel and southern routes being denied them by France. The seas around Orkney, too, were plagued by French and American privateers as Sir Walter Scott discovered when he visited the Flow during a cruise with the Lighthouse Commissioners in 1814. Even on this northern route convoys needed naval protection and a safe harbour where both warships and merchantmen, sometimes as many as a hundred sail, could assemble.

By 1808 these convoys between Longhope and Gothenburg in Sweden were running on a monthly basis, with feeder convoys from the Mersey and the Clyde.

The building of two Martello Towers, the most northerly in Britain, and an eight-gun battery to defend Longhope and the merchant fleet, started in 1813 but was not completed until 1816 - a year after the Battle of Waterloo and the end of hostilities. Such initial unpreparedness and late completion of defences were to become part of a familiar pattern in the establishment of a naval base at Scapa.

The New Menace

By the end of the 19th century Germany had become the European menace rather than Britain's hitherto traditional enemy, France. The British Navy, sensing accurately, if unwillingly, that the North Sea would now become its main theatre of operations rather than the English Channel, began using Orkney harbours much more frequently, finding in the process that the Flow was particularly suitable, not only as a commodious and safe anchorage, but also for exercising large formations of ships in sheltered water.

Up to, and indeed for some time after the outbreak of war in 1914, however, Scapa Flow's only defences were those provided by nature, narrow entrance channels protected by turbulent tides, stormy weather and savage rocks. These had provided adequate protection in the age of sail and even during the early days of steam and so it was thought, or at least hoped, they would still deter attack by the admittedly more powerful and manoeuvrable modern surface vessels as well as the new underwater craft, the submarines. Some authorities were even doubtful as to whether such sophisticated craft could reach the Flow at all from Germany.

And, of course, there was as yet no danger from the air although the Navy itself had brought up two heavier-than-air machines in a primitive carrier in 1913. Balloons and airships had been seen in Orkney skies even before that. Indeed, in 1910 two Germans became the first human beings ever to reach Orkney by air when their balloon which had gone aloft from near Munich for a pleasure trip to Switzerland or France was blown off course. Some 1500 miles and 30 harrowing hours later, much of the time over an unfriendly North Sea, they were lucky enough to crash-land in the dark near Kirkwall just avoiding being swept on out into the Atlantic.

Right up until 1914 there was much high-level naval and political debate as to what status the Flow should have - what kind of base it should be - if indeed it was to be used by the Navy at all to any great extent in time of war. Sea-going naval officers had little doubt as to its value. Such a large area of sheltered water off the North of Scotland with easy access to the Atlantic and especially to the North Sea, now under a rapidly growing threat of

German naval domination, made Scapa Flow strategically the ideal harbour for Britain's fighting fleet.

The chairborne Navy at the Admiralty, however, was not so sure. Orkney was a long way from Whitehall and on the wrong side of the Pentland Firth. With no direct rail or road link supplies would be difficult - everything would have to be transported by sea even if it were only the short distance across the Pentland Firth. The administrators regarded it as a logistical nightmare while some of the more thrusting strategists such as the First Lord of the Admiralty, Winston Churchill, would have preferred a base nearer the potential enemy, the Forth perhaps, or even the Humber.

But time was running out. The sea-going Navy won the day. Scapa Flow was to be the Grand Fleet's main strategic base throughout the war and in August 1914 that is where it was. But even at this late hour there were still no defences on the land, no booms, no minefields and no guns, only pegs in the ground showing where coast defence batteries should be sited, pegs placed there over the years by successive survey teams one of which had included Prince Louis of Battenberg, a future Commander-in-Chief Atlantic Fleet and who was First Sea Lord in 1914 when war actually came. He was father of Earl Mountbatten who commanded destroyers in Scapa Flow during World War II and who subsequently became Supreme Commander South East Asia and the last Viceroy of India.

World War I

A fine stretch of water . . . the centre and pivot of
the whole naval side of the war.

ADMIRAL VISCOUNT JELLICOE
The Grand Fleet 1914-16

1914-1915

On the outbreak of World War I Admiral Sir John Jellicoe took over command of the Grand Fleet from an elderly and allegedly ailing Admiral Sir George Callaghan and like him was appalled by the inadequacy of the Scapa defences. Only a few light guns landed from the Fleet itself covered the main entrances to the anchorage. To seaward a constant patrol of destroyers had to be maintained.

There were over 100 ships in the Flow when war was actually declared on 4 August 1914, most of them anchored off the northern shore close to the Base HQ at Scapa Pier, near Kirkwall. Some three months later in October 1914 the Base moved south across the Flow to Longhope, and the Fleet itself to moorings not far away off Flotta where they both remained for the duration. Lyness did not become the Base HQ until 1919 after the war had ended.

Royal Marines eventually took over control of the coast defence batteries and establishments from the mainly Orcadian Territorial Army gunners of the Royal Garrison Artillery, the Navy at that time preferring to defend its bases with its own personnel.

U-Boat Threat

It was soon discovered that U-boats could, in fact, reach the Flow from Germany when the cruiser *Birmingham* rammed and sank one to the east of Orkney shortly after war was declared. Jellicoe became even more apprehensive about the security of his anchorage and kept the Fleet out of it at sea for much of the first year of the war with a consequent strain on both men and machinery.

A scare on 1 September 1914 that a U-boat had managed to get into the harbour developed into what became known facetiously as the First Battle of Scapa Flow with the Fleet putting to sea in a hurry after some firing of ships' guns at what were thought to be periscopes. The Second Battle of the Flow occurred six weeks later when a U-boat was again reported as being in the harbour and again there was a lot of firing from ships as the Fleet hastily put to sea once more and this time it stayed away. No submarine had actually entered the Flow on either occasion.

Defences Grow

Coast defence guns (6 and 4.7 inch) were hurriedly being mounted at Stanger Head and Neb in Flotta, on Hoxa Head in South Ronaldsay, and at Ness near Stromness during winter 1914 and spring 1915 to cover the main entrance channels of Hoxa, Switha and Hoy Sounds.

Nineteen blockships, merchantmen like the two-funnel clipper-bowed *Thames*, were sunk across the eastern channels becoming part of the Orkney scene for the next quarter-of-a-century until being superceded by World War II defences. Anti-submarine nets were placed across the main entrances - little more than herring nets between drifters and buoys at first. Double lines of steel nets subsequently replaced these during summer 1915 as well as a barrier of steel pylons in Hoy Sound, and minefields were also laid. More blockships were sunk in the eastern approaches and underwater indicator loops were laid to give warning of any incursion by submarines or other craft. More batteries of smaller calibre guns (6- and 12-pounders) were installed in places like Holm to provide extra cover.

With the feeling of increased security engendered by these expanding defences the Fleet began to spend more time in the Flow for maintenance of its ships and training of their crews and from where it could carry out offensive sweeps across the North Sea in the hope of tempting the German High Seas Fleet to come out and fight.

Britain now had 600 naval ships building and the instruction of crews to man them became an urgent priority. Training schools were set up at Scapa which Jellicoe said had now become 'the centre and pivot of the whole naval side of the war.'

1916-1918

Jutland and After

On 30 May 1916 acting on Intelligence reports that the German High Seas Fleet had at last put to sea in force, 72 ships of the Grand Fleet anchored in Scapa Flow also weighed and by midnight had cleared Hoxa Sound heading sou'east to meet it with Jellicoe in his flagship, *Iron Duke*, leading 16 battleships, 3 battle cruisers, 4 armoured cruisers, 5 light cruisers, and 44 destroyers. They were joined at sea by 20 more ships from Invergordon and a further 52, including the new and powerful battle-cruisers, under Admiral Sir David Beatty, from the Forth - a total of 144 to meet 99 German ships. Battle was joined off Denmark west of Jutland in the afternoon of 31 May and continued through the night. Fourteen British ships with 6097 men were lost compared with the German casualties of 11 ships and 2551 men. The battle itself was indecisive, both sides claiming victory - but the fact remains that the German fleet broke off the engagement and returned to port, never to emerge again in any force until the surrender in November 1918, while the Royal Navy continued to enjoy the freedom of the seas eventually overcoming even the U-boat menace as well as tightening the North Sea blockade of Germany from Scapa at the same time.

Less than a week after the Battle of Jutland, in which she had taken part, the cruiser *Hampshire* sailed from Scapa on 5 June 1916 with Field Marshall Lord Kitchener, Britain's Minister for War, on board, bound for Russia to shore up the Czar's faltering forces beginning to crumble under German pressure.

She struck a mine laid by a U-boat off Marwick Head on Orkney's west coast during a summer gale and sank in

15 minutes. Of the 655 men on board there were only 12 survivors. Kitchener was not among them.

On 9 July 1917 the battleship *Vanguard* blew up at anchor off Flotta with the loss of nearly 1000 men - the Flow's worst disaster. The explosion was thought to have been caused by faulty ammunition.

During 1917 there were anything up to 123 warships, including 28 capital ships, 9 cruisers, 57 destroyers and 25 submarines as well as auxiliaries, using the Flow where they were joined by six dreadnoughts of the 6th Battle Squadron of the United States Navy in December 1917 - all now coming under overall operational command of Admiral Sir David Beatty, Jellicoe having moved to the Admiralty the previous year.

While operating out of the Flow the battleship *New York,* wearing the flag of Rear Admiral Hugh Rodmer, C-in-C US 6th Battle Squadron, was attacked and slightly damaged by a U-boat to the west of Orkney. The Americans retaliated with depth charges and claimed a kill.

But for the last few months of the war, from April 1918 onwards, Rosyth on the Forth became the Fleet's main base although its ships were still frequent visitors to the Flow where the defences were maintained and even increased with the construction of the air station at Swanbister.

On 28 October 1918, just two weeks before the war ended, the German submarine *UB 116* with a crew of 37 men on board made a last desperate bid to penetrate the Scapa defences. She was detected on the indicator loops and allowed to get as far as the controlled minefields in Hoxa Sound where she was blown up with the loss of all hands. It was believed to be the only occasion on which a submarine had been destroyed in a controlled minefield.

Growth of Air Power

The Flow's first air station was established on Scapa Bay in August 1914 when three seaplanes and two land planes arrived by cattle-boat and were unceremoniously dumped in a field of green oats not far from the Base HQ which was then centred round Scapa Pier. The station was built up round them. Scapa Bay, however, was not really suitable as an air base owing to the great expanse of sand at low water making the launching and retrieving of seaplanes very difficult.

A new station was built further west along the coast at Houton but did not become operational until 1917. It was sheltered and had no tidal problems. Seaplanes, flying boats and balloons operated from it and a subsidiary station was established on the Stenness Loch which became operational in 1918 but was not really satisfactory owing to shallow water, reefs and cross-winds.

Work was started on yet another air station at Swanbister not far from Houton but, like many other Scapa Flow defence projects, it was only completed after the war had ended. It was never operational.

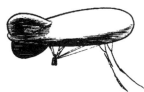

An airship and kite balloon station was established at Caldale just outside Kirkwall in 1916 mainly for servicing the balloons towed by ships. Kite balloons, not unlike the barrage balloons of World War II, but with observers in open baskets slung below them were towed aloft by both warships and merchantmen for spotting enemy submarines and mines. Strangely enough they were not particularly affected by windy conditions but were very vulnerable to electric storms - on one occasion in the Flow no fewer than 17 caught fire simultaneously and fell into the sea, fortunately with no loss of life. The airships were dirigibles, nicknamed 'blimps', also used for U-Boat spotting.

The 25-knot Cunard liner *Campania* worked up in the Flow after being converted into an aircraft carrier in April 1915 and went to sea with the Fleet on exercises where her aircraft were used for gunnery target-spotting and reconnaissance. The big drawback, of course, was that her planes after being flown off had either to come down in the sea and be hoisted aboard again or then to make for the nearest airfield if it was within range. A better and safer way of getting aircraft back to their parent ship was essential if warplanes and fighting ships were to co-operate to the best advantage in action.

After much planning and the re-design of selected ships the problem was finally resolved on 5 August 1917, when Commander Edwin Dunning flying a Sopwith Pup achieved what had hitherto been impossible by bringing his tiny single-engined biplane safely down on to the flight deck of *Furious*, a battlecruiser modified while under construction to become an aircraft carrier. When he landed she was steaming at 30 knots across the Flow. Sadly, Commander Dunning was killed shortly afterwards while attempting a second landing on *Furious*.

Before hauling down his flag as C-in-C Grand Fleet and moving to the Admiralty in November 1916, Jellicoe made a 15-minute flight over the Flow in one of the airships from Caldale.

Northern Patrol

During the period 1914-1918 there were always 10 ships patrolling between Iceland and Orkney (700 miles, 1120 km) and between Orkney and Norway (300 miles, 480km) on contraband control, their headquarters being in the commandeered Kirkwall Hotel. They were usually armed merchantmen supported by up to 15 cruisers and 20 destroyers from the Grand Fleet at Scapa. During the war they intercepted at sea some 15,000 neutral and enemy merchant ships, suspect vessels being brought into Kirkwall examination anchorage for more detailed investigation. Only 4%, it was claimed, managed to slip through the blockade.

American ships were among those intercepted up until 6 April 1917 when the United States entered the war against Germany. One of them was the *Oscar II* chartered by the multi-millionaire car manufacturer, Henry Ford, of Model T fame, heading his own ill-conceived 'Peace Mission' which came to nothing when its members fell out among themselves on reaching Oslo in neutral Norway. They had not been allowed ashore in Orkney.

German Fleet Interned

Following the Armistice on 11 November 1918 the German High Seas Fleet surrendered to the Allies off the Firth of Forth on 20 November and was ordered north to Scapa Flow for internment, the first ships, mainly destroyers, arriving under escort three days later on the 23rd. Within a week all 70 dirty and disarmed ships, many of them with mutinous crews, had dropped anchor in the Flow. The capital ships and cruisers were moored off Cava with the smaller craft in Gutter Sound, to await the outcome of the Versailles Peace Conference. The total was brought to 74 a few weeks later with the arrival of the battleship *Baden* and three smaller vessels.

The crews bringing this demoralised fleet across from Germany had numbered some 20,000 men but this figure was rapidly scaled down to only 1700 by June 1919. They had to be victualled and supplied direct from Germany. Crews were not allowed ashore nor to visit other interned ships and British personnel did not go aboard them except on official duty. There was no radio communication with Germany, the only direct contact with the Fatherland being through letters carried by the infrequent supply ships. Even Admiral Ludwig von Reuter, Commander of the Interned Fleet, on his flagship, the cruiser *Emden*, had to rely on four-day-old copies of 'The Times' newspaper from London for news of what was happening in the outside world. And his humiliated ships were under constant surveillance by Royal Navy destroyers and patrol vessels with the British First Battle Squadron of seven battleships anchored nearby in reserve.

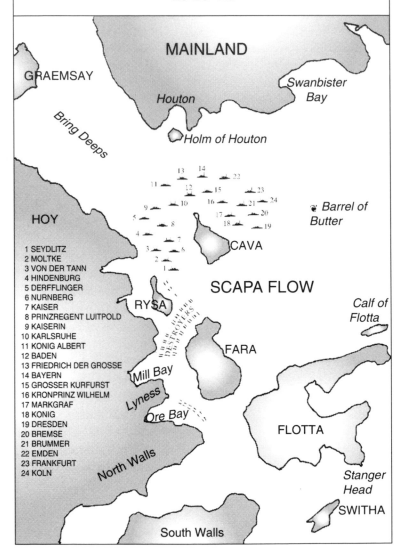

Interned German Fleet

Scapa Flow
1918-19

MAINLAND

GRAEMSAY

Houton

Swanbister
Bay

Bring Deeps

Holm of Houton

13 14
11   12   15   22
9   10   16   23
5   8   17   21   24
4   18   20
3   6   19
2
1

Barrel of
Butter

HOY

CAVA

SCAPA FLOW

1 SEYDLITZ
2 MOLTKE
3 VON DER TANN
4 HINDENBURG
5 DERFFLINGER
6 NURNBERG
7 KAISER
8 PRINZREGENT LUITPOLD
9 KAISERIN
10 KARLSRUHE
11 KONIG ALBERT
12 BADEN
13 FRIEDRICH DER GROSSE
14 BAYERN
15 GROSSER KURFURST
16 KRONPRINZ WILHELM
17 MARKGRAF
18 KONIG
19 DRESDEN
20 BREMSE
21 BRUMMER
22 EMDEN
23 FRANKFURT
24 KOLN

RYSA

DESTROYERS

FARA

Calf of
Flotta

Mill Bay

Lyness

Ore Bay

FLOTTA

North Walls

Stanger
Head

SWITHA

South Walls

The Scuttle

Sometime in May 1919 von Reuter learned belatedly from 'The Times', the probable terms of the Peace Treaty for the German Navy. They were harsh. It was to be cut to 15,000 men and 1,500 officers, 6 battleships of not more than 10,000 tons, 6 cruisers of up to 6000 tons, 12 destroyers, no U-boats, no aircraft - and the interned ships were apparently to be divided up among the Allies. The Treaty was due to be signed on 21 June the Allies having issued an ultimatum that if Germany did not accept their terms by that date hostilities would be resumed.

An officer of the old school, von Reuter remembered the Kaiser's edict that no German warship was to fall into enemy hands, and fearing a pre-emptive boarding of his defenceless ships by the British, he resolved to scuttle them on the day the Treaty was to be signed in Versailles - Midsummer Day.

Stating his only source of information to be 'The Times', four days old when it arrived on his flagship, he claimed to have been unaware that the signing of the Treaty had, in fact, been postponed for two days until 23 June. On Saturday, 21 June, the British First Battle Squadron stationed in the Flow having conveniently put to sea for an exercise to the west, von Reuter therefore duly hoisted the pre-arranged signal which ordered all his ships to be scuttled by their own crews.

First to turn over and sink just after midday was the *Friedrich der Grosse*, flagship of the High Seas Fleet at Jutland. The rest soon followed and by late afternoon 52 of them were on the bottom in anything up to 80 feet (24 m) or more of water. The others, including one battleship, a few cruisers and some destroyers, were either beached or ran aground in shallows. Last to go down was the massive *Hindenburg*, once pride of the Kaiser's navy, the only capital ship to sink on an even keel, the others having capsized under the weight of their superstructures and heavy guns as they went down. Ironically von Reuter's own flagship, the cruiser *Emden* was one of the few ships which did not sink before she beached.

The few British guard ships left in the Flow were quite inadequate to prevent the mass scuttle and the First Battle Squadron rushing back from its abandoned exercise arrived too late to do more than save a few smaller ships from sinking.

Nine German sailors lost their lives either drowned or shot. The rest, including von Reuter himself, now officially became prisoners-of-war and were shipped south to detention centres in England that same night.

There was, and still is, considerable doubt as to whether the British government knew what was going to happen and had connived at the undoubtedly very convenient scuttle. The division of the German fleet among the victorious Allies would obviously have been a diplomatic minefield.

Between the Wars

They shall beat their swords into ploughshares, and
their spears into pruninghooks . . .

SONG OF SOLOMON

North Sea Mine Barrage

To intensify the blockade and close North Sea access to Germany even more securely, the British and United States Navies had laid a barrage of 70,263 mines, each containing 300 lb (136 kg) of high explosive, covering an area of sea 240 x 25 miles (384 x 40 km) between Orkney and Utsire in neutral Norway during the summer of 1918. It was completed just before the Armistice in November 1918.

Six months later in April 1919 the two navies began to sweep the mines up again. USN ships based on Kirkwall swept the western sector in which they had laid the lion's share of 56,611 mines and the Royal Navy, working from bases further south, swept the Norwegian side. The Americans had 83 ships and 5000 men under command of Rear Admiral Joseph Strauss in his flagship *Black Hawk* operating out of Kirkwall Bay during the hazardous six-month-long operation which was completed by September 1919. The two Navies had between them cleared the 6000 square miles (15,540 sq km) of the North Sea of its deadly total of 9500 tons (9652 tonnes) of high explosive. And so the Americans, only 2000 of whom had been able to celebrate Independence Day on the Fourth of July ashore, the other 3000 being at sea, could sail home for a real Thanksgiving Day party at the end of November.

1919-1939

ACOS (Admiral Commanding Orkney and Shetland) hauled down his flag on 15 February 1920 and not long afterwards in November 1920 Scapa ceased to be even a Secondary Naval Base, the SNO (Senior Naval Officer) North of Scotland, who replaced ACOS being based at Invergordon. A naval presence was maintained, however, throughout the 1920s and 30s either by single vessels or the Home Fleet itself, with sometimes as many as 36 ships, on summer cruises when their regattas were often held in the Flow.

During the same period RAF seaplanes and flying boats carried out flights over and around the Flow prospecting possible emergency bases while civil aircraft pioneering trans-Atlantic routes often used it as a jumping off area - mainly from Houton. In 1933 Orkney's own commercial air service to the Scottish mainland started up and soon after was operating Britain's first internal air mail.

Protracted negotiations with an uncooperative Admiralty over raising the blockships and re-opening the eastern channels into the Flow for merchant and fishing vessels went on until 1931 and were never satisfactorily concluded, many of the hulks remaining in position until 1939 especially in Holm Sound.

By contrast the coast defence batteries were dismantled and their guns dismounted or broken up for scrap within months of the end of hostilities.

Raising of the German Fleet

Immediately after the scuttle of the German Fleet in 1919 the Admiralty salvaged several of the more accessible ships including the beached 28,000-ton *Baden,* some of the salvaged ships going to France.

The first civilian salvage operation was carried out by a syndicate of Stromness businessmen who bought a destroyer, raised her and towed her to what was known as the Reclamation at the north end of Stromness Harbour in 1921 where they broke her up for scrap.

A Lerwick firm headed by J. W. Robertson, Convener of Shetland County Council, also raised several other destroyers between 1923 and 1925.

But the really big salvage enterprise got under way in 1924 when the London firm of engineers and shipbreakers, Cox & Danks, then based at Queensborough in Kent, bought 26 destroyers and two capital ships from the Admiralty. All the destroyers were raised by 1926 using a German floating dock bought by Ernest Cox, a brilliant and autocratic engineer who soon became one of the world's leading salvage experts.

The first big battleship to be raised was the 23,000-ton *Moltke* in August 1927 using what was then the revolutionary new compressed-air method of lifting sunken vessels from the seabed whereby all apertures in the hull were sealed by divers where it lay. Air was then pumped into it providing the necessary buoyancy to raise the hulk from the bottom. More of the capital ships followed *Moltke* to the surface and the breakers' yards during the next few years. Only the *Hindenburg,* the one big ship to settle on an even keel, defied Cox's first attempt to raise her in 1925 but five years later backed by the experience gained with the other hulks he succeeded in refloating her too, part of the operation being watched from above by passengers and crew of the airship *Graf*

Zeppelin, the first German aircraft to fly over the Flow - but by no means the last. In December that year the *Von der Tann* was also raised. The *Prinzregent Luitpold* was much deeper than the others and an underwater internal explosion killed a salvage worker in one of the few fatal accidents to occur throughout the whole salvage of the fleet, but the difficulties were overcome and on 6 June 1931 the ship came up in a 'copy-book operation' described at the time as 'the greatest salvage feat in history', and again was honoured by a visit from her airborne compatriot, *Graf Zeppelin*, on her way across the Atlantic.

With the collapse of the scrap metal market during the early 1930s Cox gave up and from 1932 the rest of the ships were raised by Metal Industries Ltd which had already broken up some of the earlier recoveries in their yards at Rosyth on the Forth. Ironically some of the hulks were towed south by chartered German tugs flying the swastika after the Nazis came to power.

Metal Industries raised one ship a year until the outbreak of war in 1939. Last to be brought up was the 26,400-ton *Derfflinger* from a depth of 140 feet (42 m). She was towed to shallow water off Rysa near Lyness where she remained bottom-up throughout the war being towed south to the breakers' yard at Faslane on the Clyde when peace came, the *Iron Duke* preceding her a few weeks earlier also for breaking. And so these two great ships which had opposed each other at Jutland and had then lain immobile only a few miles apart in Scapa throughout the second World War came to the same sad and inglorious end together.

Threat of War Again

As Hitler and the Nazis rose to power during the 1930s the threat of another war with Germany became more than just a possibility. And should the worst happen it was almost certain that Scapa Flow would once again become a strategically important base for the Royal Navy but, just as before World War I, its defences were only the natural ones of weather, tides and rock-lined access channels inadequately augmented by the rusty remains of the World War I blockships. No guns, no booms, no minefields. These had all gone in the rush to return to peace-time conditions after the signing of the Versailles Peace Treaty in 1919.

Nevertheless Scapa was still thought, or perhaps again only hoped, to be submarine-proof. But now there was the added threat of air attack and this was recognised inasmuch that Whitehall approved the provision of 24 anti-aircraft guns for its defence. Nothing further, however, was done to supply or site them apart from a battery of eight 4.5 inch Heavy Anti-Aircraft (HAA) guns, four on either side of what was to be the Lyness Base HQ with its all-important fuel oil tanks.

As before World War I there were doubts in the Admiralty as to whether Scapa Flow was really the best place for the Navy's main strategic base in the British Isles. Was it, perhaps, too far from Germany? Or too near? Could the logistical problems of supply and reinforcement be overcome? Once again, after much high level discussion and heart-searching, the sea-going navy, who would, after all, have to use it, won the day and in 1938 it was designated a Category "A" Defended Port.

Oil tanks with a 100,000 ton storage capacity for the Fleet's fuel supply were already under construction at Lyness and tunnelling for safer underground fuel storage space in the hill behind the future Base had also started.

Work began on laying booms across the three main entrances of Hoxa, Switha, and Hoy Sounds, but there were misgivings as to whether the old WWI blockships would, in fact, provide adequate protection against U-boats or even surface craft. It wasn't, however, until war had actually been declared and the Home Fleet was in the Flow that the Admiralty finally decided to sink three more blockships across the more vulnerable eastern entrances. Sadly the vital one for Kirk Sound arrived a week too late to prevent the battleship *Royal Oak* being torpedoed and sunk at anchor inside the Flow.

During the Munich crisis of autumn 1938, in spite of having been up-graded to the status of a Category 'A' Defended Port, Scapa Flow's actual defences on the ground consisted of only the eight HAA guns of 226 Bty manned by Orkney and Caithness Territorials at Lyness and two ancient 6 inch coast defence guns at each of Stanger Head in Flotta and Ness near Stromness with a 'museum-piece' 4.7 inch destined for Neb also in Flotta. They too were to be manned by Orkney Territorials who were only recruited after the crisis was past.

The Fleet Air Arm station at Hatston on Kirkwall Bay (*HMS Sparrowhawk*), one of the first ever to have tarmac runways, was operational - but only just - and so was the obsolescent radar station at Netherbutton hurriedly moved north to the Flow from Redcar in Yorkshire. And only the boom across Hoxa Sound was actually in position, the other two being laid the following year.

World War II - 1939-1945

There is, in Orkney, an island that commands one of the entrances to Scapa Flow. There are batteries mounted on the cliff, and fulmars, riding the breeze, sail past the muzzles of the guns. Gannets with a silvery splash dive deep into the sound. On a spring morning, against the staccato coughing of anti-aircraft guns at practice, you may hear the drumming of a snipe. A crofter, ploughing his small field, must drive his plough through the shadow of a barrage-balloon. And women, coming from the byre, stand to watch a battleship go out, or destroyers with a bone in their mouth come racing in.

Ask them where they have been, and what will the answer be?

Narvik, the Denmark Strait, or anywhere between.

ERIC LINKLATER
Northern Garrisons

Inadequate Defences

The defences were very little, if at all, stronger a year after the Munich crisis on 31 August 1939, four days before the outbreak of war, when there were 44 ships of the Home Fleet already anchored in this weakly protected harbour which had been earmarked as their main home base in the event of war.

To strengthen these totally inadequate defences, especially against air attack which by this time was recognised as a really serious threat, the War Office in September 1939 produced its 'Q' Plan for the siting of 80 heavy anti-aircraft guns, 40 light anti-aircraft guns, 108 searchlights and 40 barrage balloons round the Flow.

Churchill, once again First Lord of the Admiralty, as he had been during the first war, did not much like "Q" Plan on the grounds that Britain should not dissipate its strength on 'mere passive defence' but he did approve 16 extra 3.7 inch HAA guns to thicken up the Scapa defences. He was also a strong advocate for taking the land-based defences of Scapa Flow away from the Army altogether and handing over control of them to the Royal Marines as had happened in World War I. This time he was over-ruled by the Navy itself whose top brass felt that the Army, already on the job, was better qualified and equipped for this task.

The Army's Orkney and Shetland Defences (OSDeF) had been set up on 29 September 1939, under command of Brigadier Geoffrey Kemp MC with his HQ in the Stromness Hotel, its total defences consisting of the eight HAA guns at Lyness, the five coast defence guns and their searchlights at Stanger Head and Ness, on Hoy Sound, but now reinforced by three light anti-aircraft Bofors guns at Netherbutton radar station in Holm, an infantry company (Seaforth Highlanders) and a Field Company (Royal Engineers). A little later 7 Bn Gordon Highlanders was brought in to defend 'Vital Points' and two more Field Companies Royal Engineers were drafted in to erect huts.

The Navy's Contraband Control and Northern Patrol HQ under Vice Admiral Max Horton, distinguished submarine commander of World War I, later in this war to achieve fame as C-in-C Western Approaches during the Battle of the Atlantic, was once again established in the Kirkwall Hotel as it had been in the first war and now renamed *HMS Pyramus*. Admiral Commanding Orkney and Shetland (ACOS), Admiral Sir William French, had his Base HQ aboard the old *Iron Duke* moored off Lyness and now more a floating office block than a fighting ship.

Royal Oak Torpedoed at Anchor

Just how dangerously weak the Scapa defences really were was tragically demonstrated only six weeks after the declaration of war when, during one weekend in October, the Navy lost over 800 men and two capital ships at anchor inside the Flow, one by U-boat attack, the other by Ju 88 dive-bombers of the German Air Force.

Lieut Cmdr Gunther Prien and his crew of 40 brought their *U 47* into the Flow from the North Sea through Holm Sound and Kirk Sound at high water just before midnight on Friday, 13 October. He was on the surface but no one saw him although he had of necessity to be close in to the north shore in order to pass between it and the blockships. It was a clear but dark and moonless night although the northern sky was dimly lit by the aurora borealis - or the Merry Dancers, as these 'Northern Lights' are called in Orkney.

Successfully negotiating the gaps between the blockships on the north side of Kirk Sound Prien was inside the main British naval base soon after midnight with enough torpedoes to cause havoc in the Home Fleet - had it been there. But it wasn't. Most of the ships had left the Flow the previous night. Only the *Royal Oak*, resting up after a stormy patrol outside, was at anchor off Gaitnip on the northern shore with only a few destroyers and auxiliary vessels several miles away on the other side near Lyness. She had been moored in this isolated, and, as it turned out, exposed position so that her powerful anti-aircraft armament could provide extra cover for the base if necessary.

Time was short. To make a successful escape after the attack Prien had to clear Holm Sound on the first of the ebb while there was still a sufficient depth of water - at best it would be only 59 feet (17.7 metres) at high water and *U 47* drew 31.5 feet (9.5 metres). He closed *Royal Oak*

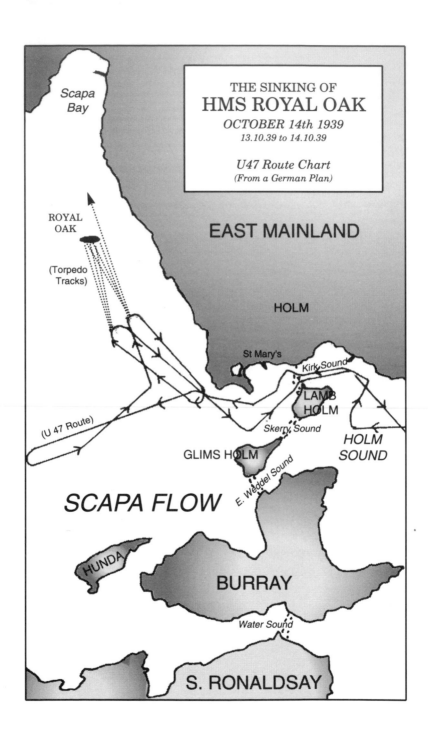

THE SINKING OF
HMS ROYAL OAK
OCTOBER 14th 1939
13.10.39 to 14.10.39

U47 Route Chart
(From a German Plan)

Scapa
Bay

ROYAL
OAK

(Torpedo
Tracks)

EAST MAINLAND

HOLM

St Mary's

Kirk Sound

LAMB
HOLM

(U 47 Route)

Skerry Sound

HOLM
SOUND

GLIMS HOLM

E. Weddel Sound

SCAPA FLOW

HUNDA

BURRAY

Water Sound

S. RONALDSAY

to 4000 yards (3600 m) and fired his bow tubes. One failed but three torpedoes were launched. There were no apparent hits but there was a small explosion forward. One torpedo may have struck obliquely and exploded without penetrating the hull or it might even have hit the anchor chain. After an investigation on board the battleship it was thought the explosion had been a minor internal one in a paint locker and the ship's company returned to their mess decks.

Prien put *U 47* about and fired his stern tubes. Again he missed. By this time the bow tubes had been re-loaded so he went about again and fired. This time the three torpedoes found their mark. Thirteen minutes later *Royal Oak* rolled over and sank in 100 feet (30 m) of water with the loss of 833 men out of a total ship's company of 1400. Many of the survivors owed their lives to the superb seamanship and courage of Skipper John Gatt and his crew on *Royal Oak's* attendant drifter, *Daisy II*, who steamed slowly alongside the stricken warship as she rolled over gathering as many survivors from the oily water as they could in the darkness.

Out at sea an hour later, having escaped, again unseen though still on the surface but this time on the south side of Kirk Sound, *U 47* dived and headed home to Germany and a hero's welcome from Hitler himself.

In Britain there was consternation both in Whitehall and at Scapa. The unbelievable had happened. For the first time a U-boat had actually penetrated the Navy's holiest of holies and had torpedoed and sunk one of its capital ships at anchor with heavy loss of life. And the blame lay squarely on the Admiralty itself for the lack of preparedness.

First Air Attack

The atmosphere of doom and gloom intensified four days later on 17 October when four of the Luftwaffe's new Ju 88 bombers dived out of the morning sun from 11,000 feet to attack the *Iron Duke,* veteran flagship of Jutland, moored off Lyness, holing her so badly by a near miss that she had to be beached and abandoned as the Naval Base HQ which now moved ashore into temporary, and at first, very inadequate accommodation. One of the bombers was shot down by the Orkney and Caithness Territorial Army gunners of 226 HAA Battery - the first enemy aircraft to be brought down by AA gunfire in Britain during World War II. But that same afternoon more bombers came back in a high level attack fortunately causing no damage although one bomb did fall in a field near the oil storage tanks at Lyness - the first to explode on British soil in this war. The German Air Force at this time, it seems, had strict orders not to drop bombs on land targets, only on ships actually at sea. This bomb at Ore farm was apparently a mistake.

The Navy now had to face the harsh reality that its Base in Scapa Flow was not only vulnerable to underwater or surface attack but that the skies above it were by no means safe either.

The first reaction was to abandon it as a base altogether or at least until it was made safer. The Fleet had, in fact, left the Flow the night before the *Royal Oak* was sunk. Now it stayed away, dispersed to various harbours round the British, mainly Scottish coast - Loch Ewe, the Clyde, the Forth, Invergordon and so on, none of which, it was now proved, could provide as good a strategic base to cover the North Sea as Scapa.

The Defence chiefs and their plans were in disarray. Work in progress, including that under 'Q' Plan, was either halted or slowed down while the whole situation was reassessed at the very highest level - Admiralty, War Office, Air Ministry and the War Cabinet. C-in-C Home Fleet, Admiral Sir Charles Forbes, remained convinced that Scapa Flow was geographically and strategically the best possible British base for his ships provided it could be adequately protected. And he carried the day. By the beginning of November it had been decided to go ahead with building up the defences at a cost of £500,000, quite a large sum in those days but very soon exceeded. An inter-Services Committee for the Defence of the Fleet Anchorage of Scapa Flow, was set up which in due course produced its 'R' Plan incorporating 'Q' Plan and augmenting it with extra coastal artillery, more booms, minefields, fighter squadrons, radar and barrage balloons.

Build-up of the Base Defences

The die having been cast there was a surge of feverish activity round the Flow. Men and materiel poured into Orkney. Guns by the dozen, both coast defence and anti-aircraft, over a hundred searchlights, radar sets for gun sites (GL), underwater steel nets and mines, barrage balloons and huts by the hundred to accommodate the massive reinforcement of troops needed to man and service them. From the Channel Coast of England they came, from the Midlands, Merseyside and Tyneside as well as from southern Scotland, plucked at a moment's notice from defence sites, often near their homes, to be dumped down on wet and windy island moors and headlands with little, and sometimes no shelter from the incessant gales, sleet, snow and rain which afflicted Orkney that first winter of the war. It was a daunting introduction to active service conditions where the perceived enemy seemed to come in the shape of hurricane-force wind driving horizontal rain and sleet before it rather than jack-booted storm troopers or Stuka dive-bombers. But at least these horrible conditions provided the hard-pressed troops with a powerful incentive to build the huts as quickly as possible even in the all-pervading mud and so get out of the wind and wet into some degree of warmth and limited comfort.

Deadline for the return of the Home Fleet to its reinforced Scapa Base was set at what was thought by many to be a rather optimistic 1 March 1940, but regardless of the appalling weather and sporadic harassment by enemy reconnaissance and mine-laying aircraft, the combined efforts of the troops came within a few days of achieving it.

Even by 6 February with less than a month to go to the deadline the original eight HAA guns at Lyness were still the only ones actually operational although another 20 had been emplaced with an extra 4000 men already landed and deployed to man them. Three weeks later by the deadline date, 1 March, 39 HAA guns, 13 LAA guns and 28 searchlights were in position and ready for action manned by a force now more than 10,000 strong, and a fortnight later still the number of guns had risen to 52 HAA thickened up by the guns of the Home Fleet which by this time had returned to its more securely defended base.

The Fleet Returns

On 8 March 1940 Winston Churchill, First Lord of the Admiralty, was on board the battlecruiser *Hood*, the Navy's largest warship, already anchored in the Flow. Five other capital ships, including the flagship, *Rodney*, in which he had sailed north from the Clyde remained out at sea to the west as it was suspected that German aircraft had mined the Hoxa entrance. Churchill had come in through what was known as the 'tradesmen's entrance', Switha Sound, in a destroyer to which he had transferred at sea from *Rodney*. On 11 March, three days later, by which time *Rodney* and the other ships, including a cruiser squadron and some 20 destroyers were safely moored in the Flow, Churchill, now back in London, was reporting to the War Cabinet that the Scapa Base was '80 per cent secure' and that any risks involved in its use by the Navy were 'acceptable'. It was probably also on this visit to welcome the Fleet back to the Flow that he gave the final go-ahead for building the anti-submarine barriers across its eastern channels which by common consent and daily usage came to bear his name.

Defences Tested

With the rapidly growing German threat to the Scandinavian countries just across the North Sea that '80 per cent security' of the Base was tested less than a week later when, as darkness fell on Saturday evening, 16 March, 14 or 15 enemy aircraft attacked the Fleet and the RNAS Hatston airfield near Kirkwall. It was the first concerted air raid since the attack in October 1939 when *Iron Duke* was holed and beached. This time about 120 high explosive bombs and some 500 incendiaries were dropped. The cruiser *Norfolk* was holed by a near miss and nine of the ship's company were killed. The Luftwaffe had by now abandoned the policy of confining air attacks exclusively to ships at sea and dropped quite a proportion of their bombs on land where the main damage was at the Brig o' Waithe on the main Kirkwall-Stromness road between the sea and the Stenness Loch. Houses were demolished and John Isbister, who lived there, was killed, becoming the first British civilian air raid casualty of the war. Why this area was singled out for attack remains a mystery - at the time there were no military targets anywhere in the vicinity.

Some 44 HAA guns of OSDeF were in action along with those of the Fleet but no hits were scored. The early warning from the obsolescent Netherbutton radar had been inadequate and some of the searchlights were not well handled. There was much heart-searching in high places and, with the security of the Scapa Base again in question, the Fleet was ordered to sea for the two nights of full moon which followed.

Barrage Introduced

For some time OSDeF had been contemplating the possibility of a radar-controlled aerial anti-aircraft barrage to put a curtain of bursting shells across the path of incoming bombers and such necessary gun-laying radar sets (GL) were now arriving at battery level. Anti-aircraft purists were not in favour. It would be a waste of ammunition, inaccurate and probably ineffective. Aimed gunfire was the only real answer, they said. It may well have been so in an ideal situation but accurate aiming was very difficult if not actually impossible in the poor-light conditions of a dusk attack such as that on 16 March 1940 especially if the searchlights were unable to illuminate the target. The Navy, however, did like the idea and with its blessing a two-minute trial barrage was fired as an exercise on 26 March 1940.

Not long afterwards, on 2 April, again as darkness fell, the barrage was tried out again, for real this time, when a dozen or so enemy aircraft attempted to bomb the growing number of ships, both transports and warships, anchored in the Flow, including some from the French Navy. They were met by 450 HAA rounds of the new barrage with only eight planes getting through and even these did not press home the attack turning away without doing any damage after only ten minutes. The embryo barrage had at least proved its worth as a deterrent even if no hits were scored.

There was a breathing space of six days until Monday, 8 April when, again at dusk, the Luftwaffe launched its third and heaviest raid against the Flow so far in 1940. Over two dozen bombers were involved and more than half of them pressed home their attack in twos and threes from 12,000 to 20,000 feet in the face of what was now an intense barrage of 2700 bursting shells from OSDeF's 81 heavy guns alone with those of the Fleet in addition. Some

15 bombs of up to 1000 lbs (450 kg) were dropped aimed mainly at the Hoxa and Switha booms. They missed and no damage was done but the guns claimed four planes shot down and RAF Hurricanes from Wick claimed at least three more. One Heinkel III hit by gunfire over the Flow crash-landed at Wick airfield, the others went down in the sea. There had been ample early warning this time with the radar-equipped cruiser *Curlew* plotting the raiders as far away as 80 miles out to sea so giving the RAF fighters time to intercept and break up the formations.

Last Big Raid

Next day, 9 April, the reason for the previous night's heavy raid became obvious - German forces had invaded Denmark and perhaps more significantly, seen from Scapa, Norway, with its airfields and sheltered ports no more than 300 miles away. No wonder they wanted to destroy the booms and make the Flow once again vulnerable to surface and underwater attack from their new Scandinavian bases. Blocking the Flow's entrances with wreckage would also delay the despatch eastwards of the Allied anti-invasion force assembled at Scapa.

They would certainly try again. But when? That Tuesday, the fateful 9 April, was a very tense day all round the Flow. But the bombers didn't come - not even at dusk. Nor did they appear at first light the following morning, Wednesday 10 April, but there was considerable enemy aerial activity by single reconnaissance aircraft over and around Orkney during the afternoon. Something very unpleasant was obviously brewing. And at a quarter to nine, out of the gathering darkness, at last they came - 60 bombers, mainly Heinkel IIIs and Ju 88s, at between 7000 and 10,000 feet, attacking from the east and sou'east. They were met by a ferocious barrage in which the land guns alone fired 1700 rounds breaking up the formations but at least 20 planes got through and once again tried, without success, to bomb the booms. There was, however, one hit on the cruiser *Suffolk* causing only superficial damage.

The OSDeF guns claimed three planes shot down and the RAF fighters accounted for another two with four more damaged. Subsequent Intelligence reports, particularly from the Navy, suggested much heavier losses by the Luftwaffe, one indeed claiming that few, if any, of their bombers returned to base. At all events the German Air Force never again attempted a serious attack on the British Fleet at anchor in the Flow apart from a very confused and haphazard incursion a fortnight later on 24 April involving 23 aircraft of which only five risked the barrage and caused no damage.

However, although there were no more concerted raids on the Flow, the Luftwaffe maintained its interest in the anchorage throughout the war with reconnaissance flights in daylight and mine-laying sorties at night concentrating mainly on the entry channels but sometimes risking a tip-and-run raid inside the Flow itself. They caused no damage to shipping, the mines being promptly and efficiently swept by the Navy. Outlying searchlight sites and small isolated radar stations were also attacked from time to time. These pin-prick sorties mostly directed at targets just outside the Flow itself had more nuisance than military value but indicated that German air crews had developed a healthy respect for the Scapa barrage.

Reaching the Peak

Scapa's defences were reaching their peak both in quantity and quality. OSDeF, now with a strength of over 11,000 men and still growing, became a Major General's command and was up-graded to the status of an infantry division with two brigades, one based in Hoy, the other on the Mainland, and its own HQ still in the Stromness Hotel. By 15 April 1940 all 88 HAA guns specified in 'R' Plan were in position and ready for action as were 32 LAA guns with four more ready for siting. There were 88 AA searchlights operational with another 14 in position awaiting spares and there were even 98 old Lewis machine guns of first war vintage on the sites for defence against low level air attack or if the worst came to the worst, in their original ground role.

Nor was coast defence against surface or underwater attack neglected. By 3 June there were 19 guns of various calibres ready for action on 14 battery positions - the four original 6 inch guns were still sited two each at Stanger Head and Ness with another two, as during WWI, now mounted at Hoxa Head in South Ronaldsay to cover, along with the Flotta guns, the vital Hoxa Sound entrance to the Flow; the ancient 4.7 gun had been moved to Neb and two more 4.7s were later sited at Rerwick Head in Tankerness and at Carness three miles to the north-east of Kirkwall, to cover the channel between Shapinsay and the Mainland, known as The String, the main entry to Kirkwall Harbour and the Contraband Control examination anchorage of the Northern Patrol. There were ten new 12-pounders, one each at Galtness in Shapinsay and Wasswick in Rendall, also covering Kirkwall Harbour, and round the Flow itself, two at Gate on Flotta and another two at Houton Head in Orphir with one each at Holm and Scad Head in Hoy. More were to follow, mainly anti-motor-torpedo-boat twin 6-pounders to cover the booms, and the numbers continued to grow.

By 1942 the entrances to the Flow and the Contraband Control anchorage to the north of Kirkwall were defended by a total of 37 guns in 22 battery positions - eleven 6 inch, seventeen 12-pounders and 11 twin 6-pounders with 52 searchlights.

These Fixed Defences, as they were termed, now had 900 gunners to man them divided into three Fire Commands with HQs in Flotta, Kirkwall and Stromness. None of their guns ever had to engage a real enemy target but they quite often had to fire 'bring-to' rounds to stop ships entering forbidden zones. Like the rest of the garrison they now had to re-train for ground attack roles both as artillery and infantry in case of invasion.

The Navy had been busy too, both on land and sea, doubling up its booms, laying controlled minefields and installing underwater detection loops as well as extending facilities ashore at Lyness where the Base HQ *(HMS Proserpine)* was now established after the bombing and beaching of *Iron Duke* in October 1939. Four of her 6 inch guns were later brought ashore and mounted, two at Carness and two at Rerwick, replacing the old 4.7s in order to strengthen the defence of the Contraband Control anchorage in Kirkwall Roads.

The RAF was building two important long-range radar stations at Start Point in Sanday and near Longhope as well as up-dating the one at Netherbutton while numerous smaller stations with more specialised functions were under construction or planned.

The RAF close-defence of the anchorage was provided by a balloon barrage to prevent low-level attack on the Fleet. Some balloons were flying as early as February 1940 but the full complement was not achieved until that summer. Even so on the first day that the stipulated 40 balloons were in the air simultaneously the Orkney climate did the dirty on them - an unexpected gale sprang up and 39 of them were quite literally gone with the wind. They were soon back in action again with replacements but the Orkney weather was always a problem - during the bad winter of 1943/44 alone, for instance, 350 balloons were lost. By 1941 the Scapa Flow Balloon Barrage became 950 Squadron with a total of 81 balloons 26 of them flying from trawlers moored round the anchorage close to the Fleet.

The more aggressive RAF air defence was provided by three fighter squadrons, mainly Hurricanes based at Wick on the other side of the Pentland Firth but operating in conjunction with the Navy's Fleet Air Arm squadrons which included some obsolescent, but still formidable, Sea Gladiator biplanes, at Hatston just outside Kirkwall. The RAF fighters were on station and operational by February 1940, one of their patrols shooting down an enemy reconnaissance plane on 2 March. The Fleet Air Arm squadrons had been operational from the outbreak of war. Later the air defence was strengthened with the addition of three new airfields in Orkney at Skeabrae for the RAF and Twatt (*HMS Tern*) for the FAA in the West Mainland and Grimsetter, now Kirkwall airport, on the east, all of them, along with the Wick-based squadrons and the OSDeF guns, coming under control of the Sector/Gun Operations Room just outside Kirkwall.

By summer 1940 Orkney was an iron-clad fortress bristling with guns ready to repel all comers whether on, over or under the sea and with invasion by the German Army from bases in Norway now more than just a remote possibility the more vulnerable beaches were obstructed by anti-tank traps and obstacles covered by hastily built concrete machine gun posts for the infantry or the Local Defence Volunteers (LDV) subsequently renamed the Home Guard. Recruiting for this volunteer part-time force opened on 19 May 1940 and within a month 300 Orcadians had enlisted, By 30 July there were over 500 of them armed with 490 rifles and 25,000 rounds of ammunition and they became the first Home Guardsmen in Scotland to go on active service when they were allocated and took up positions covering possible invasion beaches and areas where paratroops or airborne troops might land. Eventually Orkney had two Home Guard battalions, one of which recruiting most of its strength from contractors' men working on defence projects round the Flow earned the nickname of the Orkney Foreign Legion. Orkney was also one of the few, if not the only, Home Guard to have its own artillery, for a time being equipped with the famous French 75 field guns of the first war.

All this was accomplished in less than six months under the threat, indeed, reality of air attack and in what might be politely called 'adverse weather conditions', by soldiers, sailors and airmen who for the most part had been part-time amateurs only a few months before. They learned to be professionals the hard way, and fast, many even having to build their own huts for shelter - 877 in all, 749 in 10 weeks alone, an average of 10 huts a day - and in many cases without any previous knowledge of the skills required. But they soon acquired them and were ready with their guns too if the call came.

And on Christmas Day 1940 there was a bonus. The Luftwaffe sent a Ju 88 to Orkney on a reconnaissance flight to have a look at, among other things, what was happening at Skeabrae where the RAF airfield was under construction. But it was actually operational and to such an extent that three of the American-built Grumman Martlet fighters which had just landed took off again and forced the intruder to crash-land not far away. The crew were

captured and handed over to the Home Guard by the
farmer who owned the field where they had crashed and
who had, himself, then a captain in the Merchant Navy,
been taken prisoner when his ship was sunk by a German
U-boat in the Atlantic during the first World War.

The numbers engaged in Orkney on the Scapa
defences continued to rise and during 1941 following this
Christmas present of an almost undamaged Ju 88, they
peaked at 12,500 Navy personnel on the Base, 30,000
soldiers guarding it and a civilian labour force of 3700,
many of them Irish, working on defence projects, adding
up to some 46,200 to which must be added the RAF
personnel on the new airfields, the balloons and radar
stations as well as the crews of warships constantly coming
in and out of the anchorage. Altogether a grand total of
well over 50,000 men and women, more than double the
number of Orcadians living in the islands between the
wars.

The Churchill Barriers

Undoubtedly the biggest single defence project, not only militarily, but geographically and socially, was the construction of what came to be called the Churchill Barriers or Causeways, sealing off the eastern entrances to the Flow against seaborne attack either on the surface or under it.

There were four of these channels, all of them comparatively shallow and all with dangerous tide races of up to 10 knots (18.2 kph) or even 12 knots (21.8 kph) in certain conditions. Stretching south from Holm on the Orkney Mainland they ran between the smaller islands of Lamb Holm, Glims Holm, Burray and South Ronaldsay. It was through Kirk Sound between Lamb Holm and the Mainland that Prien had brought his U-boat to sink the *Royal Oak* that dark night in October 1939.

Ever since World War I, when the Admiralty first sank blockships across these channels, there had been schemes to block them more permanently but nothing had actually been done mainly because of the enormous cost involved but also because, of course, until World War I they had been in regular peace-time use by merchant ships and fishing vessels. More blockships were sunk across them in 1939 but too few and too late to save the *Royal Oak*. That disaster, however, concentrated naval and defence thinking enormously and plans for the ultimate complete closure of these loopholes emerged during the following winter. On-the-spot surveys were also carried out so that in March 1940 during his visit to welcome the Fleet back to its Scapa Base, Churchill was able to give the scheme his final blessing and, as it happened, his name.

No time was lost in getting on with the job. Work on the ground and in the water began in May 1940 and by the end of 1942 the four channels with a total width of 7400 feet (2220 m) were effectively blocked and submarine-proof. Early the following year, 1943, they were finally completely closed to surface craft as well and in 1944 traffic was using the 6 mile (9.6 km) roadway from Holm to South Ronaldsay including the 3.25 miles (5.2 km) along the top of the causeways themselves although the official opening did not take place until 12 May 1945, just after the war in Europe had ended, when the then First Lord, A.V. Alexander, performed the ceremony.

The causeways, now a permanent feature of the Orkney scene, had cost an estimated £2.5 million, probably the equivalent of £150m or £200m in the 1990s. In 1943 there were as many as 1720 men working on the project including 1200 Italian prisoners-of-war, who left a lasting memorial to their Orkney incarceration in the Italian Chapel on Lamb Holm which they built out of two Nissen huts and odd scraps of metal to remind them of their sunnier and warmer homeland. The average number of men engaged at any one time, however, was 1270, of which 920 were Italians, the others being mainly civilian workers employed by the contractors, Balfour Beatty & Company.

And in addition to the building of the barriers themselves the project had meant the construction of three piers, three hutted camps, five generating stations and the erection of four huge cable-ways across the channels to service the work. It had also involved the opening of seven new quarries to supply the material needed for the 'bolsters' of rubble and the 5- and 10-ton concrete blocks used in the construction.

By the time the Barriers were completed, of course, the danger of a seaborne attack was long past but they have been a boon ever since to the social and economic life of the islands as indeed have two of the wartime airfields. Hatston became for a time Orkney's main civil airport before the other RNAS and RAF airfield at Grimsetter was demobilised to become the present Kirkwall Airport.

Hatston is now Kirkwall's Industrial Estate and for a few years after the war its naval hutting provided temporary housing for the town.

At the Peak

Although the Scapa Defences had reached a peak of readiness and efficiency by 1941 the garrison could by no means rest on its laurels. With the enemy only 300 miles away in Norway the possibility of invasion or at least of commando-type raids could not be ignored. Reconnaissance flights by the Luftwaffe were frequent as were occasional bombing, machine gunning and minelaying sorties by single or small groups of aircraft. These forays, however, were usually on softer targets just outside the Flow itself. Lighthouses like Auskerry to the east were attacked or the radar station under construction on Sanday in the North Isles where a civilian was killed. But quite early in 1941 a lone Ju 88 did get through the defences to circle Flotta before being driven off by 123 HAA rounds from the island's guns; another dived out of cloud to drop a 1000 lb bomb, also on Flotta, some time later. And one dark and cloudy night, again in 1941, a particularly bold spirit came in over the Pentland Firth, shut off his engines, dived to 2500 feet over Flotta, loosed off flares, dropped two 1000 lb bombs near a gun site and shot down a barrage balloon before making good his escape. On the eastern side of the Flow a parachute mine, probably intended for one of the channels later blocked by the Churchill Barriers, actually landed in Burray blowing the doors and windows out of a farmhouse but causing no serious injuries. A farmer in Holm was less fortunate when parts of his steading were demolished by a stray bomber and he was himself seriously injured. Stromness and the naval airfield at Hatston on the outskirts of Kirkwall, where another civilian was killed, were also machine-gunned as were isolated searchlight sites and smaller radar stations.

The daily and nightly routine of constant watch and ward could never be relaxed while training, training and still more training went on continuously with 'war games' against the day when such exercises might become reality.

Reinforcements of men and materiel like the new Z batteries with their 64 primitive rocket launchers to defend key installations against low level air attack, continued to be deployed right into mid-1943 by which time Hitler's self-inflicted embroilment in Russia was to some extent easing the immediate pressure in the West where the build-up for the Second Front had begun.

Nor was the Navy idle. Ships of the Home Fleet were constantly on the move in and out of the Flow on such routine but nonetheless hazardous missions as the escort of Arctic convoys to Murmansk in northern Russia or the more spectacular tracking down and sinking of the powerful German battleship, *Bismarck,* whose break for the Atlantic via Norway was discovered and reported to the C-in-C Home Fleet in Scapa by a naval aircraft from Hatston.

And after being housed in temporary and often inadequate hutted accommodation ever since the *Iron Duke* was bombed and beached in October 1939, Base HQ and

Communications Centre *(HMS Proserpine)* at Wee Fea near Lyness was completed, occupied and operational by 1943 with 230 of the Women's Royal Naval Service (WRNS) handling anything up to 8800 signals a day by telephone, teleprinter and radio to and from ships and shore stations world-wide. The main buoys in the anchorage were also connected so that incoming vessels such as the C-in-C's flagship could pick up their moorings and speak direct to Whitehall or wherever on a secure telephone line.

The nearby underground 100,000-ton-capacity (101,000 tonnes) fuel oil tanks tunnelled into the hill behind the Base were completed and filled the same year augmenting the more vulnerable above-ground tanks of similar capacity already in use at Lyness near the 600 foot (180 m) harbourage dubbed the 'Golden Wharf' because of its rumoured enormous, but undisclosed, final cost. With a depth alongside of 29 feet (8.7 m) it handled close on 100,000 tons of stores in its first year of operation. Some of the tunnelling for the underground tanks had been carried out by Norwegian miners from the Spitzbergen coal pits brought out by the Navy during a raid on those Arctic islands.

Two more 'ships' had been 'launched' to join *HMS Proserpine* at Lyness, *HMS Sparrowhawk* at Hatston and *HMS Pyramus* at Kirkwall. Unlike these other 'stone frigates' ashore, *HMS Pleiades* was actually afloat in the shape of the former Union Castle liner, *Dunluce Castle*. Moored off Lyness she was the Base depot ship and terminus for the Pentland Firth naval ferry service providing accommodation for sailors awaiting their own ships and in addition she was HQ for the hundred or so drifters and trawlers requisitioned with their crews mainly from northeast Scottish fishing ports. They were the workhorses of the Base, constantly fetching, carrying and patrolling as their predecessors had done in World War I. *Pleiades* also controlled the fleets of small boats and

launches needed by the Navy and the regular two-hourly
ferry service round the Flow used by service people and
civilians alike and which continued for nearly 12 years in a
modified form even after the war ended.

HMS *Pomona*, on shore at Lyness, was Boom Defence
Command HQ with its 6.5 miles (10.4 km) of steel nets and
buoys looked after and kept in repair by the 16 sturdy,
long-snouted ships which also opened and closed the
boom 'gates' for the passage of their more glamorous big
sisters into and out of the safety of the anchorage.

But as the tides of war moved further away to Russia,
the Western Desert and the Far East with the build-up for
D-Day gaining momentum further south at home, the
strategic emphasis of the war shifted and the probability of
direct action on land and even in the air gradually began to
recede from Scapa and the troops now had to face a more
insidious enemy - boredom. To combat this menace
garrison theatres and cinemas in Stromness, Lyness, Flotta,
Kirkwall and Holm as well as on gunsites and hutted
camps right round the Flow provided entertainment of all
kinds from concerts of classical music and plays to
knockabout variety shows by famous artistes from concert
hall, theatre or radio like Yehudi Menuhin, Gracie Fields,
or Tommy Handley and by the troops themselves among
whom there was a wealth of talent, both professional and
amateur. There were educational courses, lectures and
discussion groups, plenty of reading material including the
garrison's own weekly newspaper, the 'Orkney Blast'
complete with 'pin-ups', to keep them abreast of what was
going on, not only in Orkney, but in the wider world
outside. Some units took up gardening in a big way, there
were dances somewhere nearly every night and plenty of
sport, football in particular. And, of course, on the purely
military side there were field exercises and constant
training for the garrison could not lower its guard even
though the threat of attack now looked less imminent.

Readiness and efficiency had to be maintained at the highest pitch.

Leave, or lack of it, assumed significant importance in the troops' minds and crossing off the days on the calendar until it came round again was a hopeful if sometimes frustrating pastime. When it did come there were still the seasick miseries of the Pentland Firth to be endured on the troopships, *Earl of Zetland* for the Army from Stromness, or the *St Ninian* for naval personnel from Lyness, before boarding the nightly troop train, known like its predecessor in the first war as 'The Jellicoe', for the long haul from Thurso to Euston. An arduous, crowded and uncomfortable 700 mile journey - but after six tedious months guarding the Flow they thought it was well worth it.

The summer of 1943 saw the first reduction in the garrison strength when a few searchlight batteries were withdrawn and not replaced. With the advance of radar controlled anti-aircraft gunnery they were becoming redundant in any case. But in February 1944 the withdrawal of the HAA guns themselves began as troops were drafted south to back up the imminent D-Day landings. And soon after that the barrage balloons went south to cope with the flying bomb attacks on London.

By January 1945 as the Allies in Europe were poised ready to invest Germany itself all the rest of the HAA guns and searchlights round the Flow were taken out of action and their troops sent south. Only a few LAA batteries were retained just in case of a kamikaze-type attack as had happened in October 1918 when the *UB 116* had made an unsuccessful last-minute suicide bid to breach the Flow's underwater defences.

According to official statistics the civilian air-raid sirens had wailed their warning 65 times during the war although most people felt they had heard them far more often than that. It was also recorded that 16 air attacks had actually taken place on land targets in which a total of 288 high explosive bombs, some thousands of incendiaries, and two parachute mines had been dropped on Orkney soil killing three civilians and seriously wounding 11 more. Quite a number of buildings had been damaged or destroyed mainly in the country areas when the enemy planes had either missed their military targets or had jettisoned their bombs rather than face the Scapa barrage. Fortunately the civilian Air Raid Precaution (ARP) Wardens and rescue services, who had been on active duty since before the war began, never had to cope with a major incident but, as these figures show, with a prime target like the Home Fleet anchored right in their midst they had to be prepared for anything the enemy might throw at the islands.

After VE-Day there was a rapid dismantling of the remaining defences but this time the guns were not destroyed or broken up as after the first war but stored and eventually shipped south. Huts were sold off by the hundred, some of them going to France, for housing, and in Orkney itself there were plenty of buyers. Scratch the outer walls of many one-storey houses in Orkney today, including my own, and you will often find the original army hut round which it was built. Several of the hutted camps in or near the two towns were taken over by the local authorities to serve as temporary housing.

Peace at Last

. . . .The tumult and the shouting dies;
The Captains and the Kings depart.

RUDYARD KIPLING
Recessional

Back to Civvy Street

VE-Day, 8 May 1945, came wet and dull in Orkney but with the feeling of relief that it was all over - well, nearly all over. The war against Japan was still raging in the Far East and the Orcadians of 226 HAA Bty were now in action against the Japanese in Burma often using their guns against land targets rather than aircraft. For them, and those they had left behind in Orkney, the war would not be over for several months yet. And for the troops still in Orkney there was a feeling of anti-climax as they waited for posting or demob.

When peace finally came after the Japanese surrender on 15 August 1945 (VJ-Day) and Orcadians could at last look forward with confidence to the safe return of their own service men and women, they still had many 'strangers within their gates' in the shape of Italian prisoners-of-war, units of the Polish Army and the remnants of the garrison itself now engaged in closing-down and clearing-up operations. In January 1946 a very much reduced OSDeF HQ, now only a Brigadier's command, moved from the Stromness Hotel to the empty huts vacated by the Navy at Hatston. The following year with more and more troops returning to civilian life, it was reduced still further and renamed OSGAR (Orkney and Shetland Garrison), a Lieut Colonel's command.

The Flow itself, with its periphery of derelict gun sites, their rusting Nissen huts already beginning to rattle in the autumn gales, was still a naval base though on a greatly reduced scale. ACOS had, in fact, hauled down his flag as early as March 1945 to be replaced by a C-in-C

(Ashore) and subsequently by an even lowlier Resident
Naval Officer (RNO), usually a Commander.

Naval ships in ones and twos such as the minesweepers clearing the North Sea and the Atlantic still used
the anchorage from time to time mainly to re-fuel at the
Lyness Oil Depot but occasionally bigger ships arrived as in
1948 when the two battleships *Howe* and *Anson* along with
the cruiser *Superb* and four destroyers dropped anchor for a
few days. Britain's largest capital ship of the day, the 42,000
ton *Vanguard*, with a cruiser and destroyer escort also used
the Flow during several summer cruises between 1950 and
1954 anchoring off Flotta close to where the remains of her
ill-fated namesake still lie on the seabed. Her visit in June
1954 was, in fact, the last time a battleship of the Royal Navy
was seen in the Flow for they were now, in the atomic age,
an endangered species on the point of extinction and it was
only a few years before she, too, was 'mothballed' and
finally broken up without ever having fired a shot in anger.

Scapa's days as a naval base were now numbered. In
1956 the Ministry of Defence announced its imminent
closure as part of the £100 million economy cuts. And the
blow finally fell on 29 March 1957, a cold grey blustery day
in early spring, when for the last time at Lyness the White
Ensign was hauled down in the traditional naval 'Sunset'
ceremony and with it also came fluttering down the 266-
foot-long Paying Off Pennant - one foot for every month
that the Boom Defence Base, the only surviving HQ at
Scapa, had been in commission. And appropriately, if
rather sadly, the only naval craft alongside the Golden
Wharf was a humble boom defence ship, *HMS Barleycorn*,
whose services in the Flow were now no longer needed. It
was truly the end of an era in British naval history

Hard Times Ahead?

It was a sad day, too, for the people of Orkney's South Isles, especially those in Hoy, Walls and Flotta for whom the Base and the earlier salvage depot at Lyness had not only provided reasonably well-paid work but were social centres as well. Even after the war some 125 local people had still been directly employed at the Base with many others earning their living in associated service industries. And this time there was no scuttled German fleet to provide years of salvage work for Orcadians as after the first war, only the rusting hulks of redundant blockships and a few other wrecks.

Seven ships, the three battleships, *Konig, Kronprinz Wilhelm* and *Markgraf* with the four light cruisers, *Brummer, Karlsruhe, Koln* and *Dresden,* still lie on the bottom. Their depth made re-floating both impracticable and uneconomic. From time to time some salvage has been carried out piecemeal on them as they lie on the seabed but now they are mainly a tourist attraction for sport divers.

They were worked on sporadically by various salvage firms, most of them being broken up where they lay rather than being raised. Along with redundant material collected from sites ashore they produced some 9300 tons of valuable scrap metal some of it going back to Germany for the manufacture of, among other things, razor blades. It was also found that the high quality steel in the remaining WWI German ships had an unexpected extra value. Having lain well down below the surface of the Flow for more than 40 years their armour-plating had not been contaminated by the radiation emitted into the atmosphere during the atmospheric testing of nuclear bombs just after the war. As a result this metal was particularly suitable for the manufacture of medical and surgical instruments where radiation-free material was essential. But by 1954 this vein had been pretty well worked out. Too few reasonably accessible hulks remained to attract economic salvage operations on any scale and so there was little or no prospect of long-term employment for local people brought up in this tradition. The outlook was bleak indeed. The population of North and South Walls where most of them lived nearly halved in the ten years between 1951 and 1961 dropping from 844 to 455, and in nearby Flotta the drop was from 255 to 123 as they were forced to seek work elsewhere.

Ships of the NATO navies came in from time to time as the Cold War intensified and occasional exercises, some of them involving beach landings of troops and parachute drops, were held but these visits provided no permanent work.

Advent of Oil

Although the Royal Navy has now left Scapa Flow, the anchorage remains and its strategic importance is undiminished. Modern naval warfare, with its computer technology and advanced weapons and sensors together with its integrated afloat support, bears little resemblance to that of forty years ago. However today, in Scapa, it is oil that must be protected and ships must still have shelter; so the Flow is as important as ever.

ADMIRAL SIR JOCK SLATER, GCB, LVO,
Chief of Naval Staff and First Sea Lord
Foreword to
This Great Harbour Scapa Flow

North Sea Bonanza

It was not until 1969 with the discovery of oil under the North Sea that light began to glimmer, not so much at the end of the tunnel, as at the outflow of a pipeline. The American-based Occidental consortium of oil companies was formed in 1971 to exploit any possible finds to the east of Orkney. Two years later in 1973 they had a successful strike 135 miles southeast of the Flow. Orkney was flooded with would-be entrepreneurial oilmen looking for sites where it might be profitably brought ashore.

The Flow with its sheltered water was a popular and obvious choice and Orkney County Council, later to become Orkney Islands Council, took prompt measures to ensure it retained control over any such development, particularly around the Flow.

Occidental having established that there was a potential 708 million barrels of extractable oil in what they now called the Piper and Claymore fields, chose Flotta as the place to bring it ashore. An oilman's 'barrel' works out at about 34 Imperial gallons or 154 litres.

Once again there was a surge of feverish, almost frenetic, activity in the Flow and outside it as the 135-mile-long pipelines were laid in unfriendly waters and the Flotta terminal with its huge storage tanks, jetties and single-point moorings where tankers could load, were under construction ashore at an estimated cost of $650 million. The associated Piper and Claymore rigs out in the North Sea were also being built at a cost of another $12,657 million. There was no shortage of work now, and better still, there was the prospect of longer-term employment when the terminal became operational which it did after three years of intense activity almost to the day of that first strike. In December 1976 oil began to flow from the Piper field 135 miles (216 km) out in the North Sea to Flotta and has continued to do so ever since apart from a close-down of about a year after the violent explosion in July 1988 which destroyed the Piper Alpha production rig killing 167 men - one of the worst disasters in the history of oil exploitation - and even then some oil continued to reach the terminal from smaller wells.

By the end of 1984 some 833 million barrels of oil had been brought ashore and processed at Flotta to be loaded into 1554 tankers in transit to refineries in various parts of the world. And by the end of 1994 the total of crude which has passed through the Flotta terminal since 1976 had risen to 1,703,829,844 barrels. Huge super-tankers of 200,000 tons and more now take the place of the battleships and cruisers of earlier years as they load at the single-point moorings.

All this provided steady work for as many as 300 people, about 200 of them Orcadians, a figure comparing well with the numbers employed between the wars on salvaging the German fleet. And the Harbours Department of the Orkney Islands Council, which succeeded the County Council after the reorganisation of local government, employs a considerable staff to man its pilot launches and tugs bringing in very welcome revenue to swell its Reserve Fund earmarked to help local enterprises especially against the day when, as they must, the North Sea wells run dry.

In the meantime oil continues to flow from under the North Sea into Flotta terminal's 4.5-million-barrel capacity tanks for processing and onward shipment and the flare-stack burning off surplus gas still lights up Orkney's night sky but now it is all operated by a French-controlled group, Elf Enterprise Caledonia, which acquired it from Occidental in 1991.

How long the oil will keep coming no one knows for certain but Occidental's initial forecast that Piper would run dry by 1993 has long been overtaken by events with an average of 330,000 barrels a day being handled at the Flotta Terminal in 1994 and informed estimates now suggest it may be well into the 21st century before Piper and Claymore finally cease production.

In the meantime while the throughput had dropped to between 250,000 and 280,000 barrels a day in early 1996 handled by a Flotta work-force of 370 it would be boosted by anything up to an extra 50,000 barrels a day from the MacCulloch field in the Moray Firth by the end of the year. Even more significant is the 85,000 barrels a day, the first of the Atlantic oil, due to arrive from the Foinaven field to the west of Orkney in August 1996.

At all events Scapa Flow is and always has been resilient, ready to be adapted for new uses, peaceful or otherwise, although it seems unlikely that ever again it will see such great fleets of warships as in the two World Wars or even as in Viking times, but as long as ships sail the northern seas they will always find shelter from storm and tempest with safe holding ground in this great harbour.

. . . And Now

After three major upheavals in a century - two world wars and the oil boom - the Flow has now returned to its placid normality - or very nearly.

Utilitarian tankers have replaced the sinister elegance of the warships, pleasure craft and the occasional cruise liner ride its waves and fishermen look for catches in its sheltered waters while all the time the oil terminal hums with activity.

But apart from those new-look ships and the Flotta flare-stack the Flow itself looks much the same today as it has done throughout history and before. The smooth contours of the hills, the silhouetted islands and the wide waters of the great harbour would be as familiar to the Norsemen of the tenth century as to the bluejackets of the two world wars or the oilmen of today. There have, of course, been changes. The permanent closing of the eastern channels has made it more of an inland sea than ever with resultant changes in the movement of the tides.

Scars of two wars - gun emplacements, camp-sites and suchlike - moulder into the landscape taking their place alongside the monuments of earlier times like the Hoxa burial mound of Thorfinn Skull-splitter who ruled Orkney a thousand years ago. The Lyness oil-tanks have been demolished except for one retained as part of the Visitor Information Centre telling the Scapa story with displays and relics of the wars.

Now, once again, the varied wildlife of the islands has the freedom of the Flow and its shores - seals, whales and dolphins in the sea and mountain hares on the Hoy hills. V-formation skeins of wild-geese are familiar sights and sounds in autumn skies when hundreds of long-tailed and other ducks also fly in to take up their winter quarters. Cormorants hang themselves out to dry in the sun and oystercatchers, redshanks and ringed plovers scurry along the sands in search of a meal.

Scapa Flow is still a busy, but happily, a more peaceful place.

For Those In Peril

But, John, have you seen the world, said he,
Trains and tramcars and sixty-seaters,
Cities in lands across the sea -
Giotto's tower and the dome of St. Peters?

No, but I've seen the arc of the earth,
From the Birsay shore, like the edge of a planet,
And the lifeboat plunge through the Pentland Firth
To a cosmic tide with the men that man it.

ROBERT RENDALL
Angle of Vision

The Lifeboat Story

No saga of Scapa Flow during the last century-and-a-half can be complete without special reference to two of its most important and honoured institutions - the Longhope and Stromness lifeboats with their dedicated crewmen.

Both stations lie on the periphery of the Flow - Stromness in the town centre itself, at the western entrance; Longhope in Brims on the Pentland Firth near the southern openings to the anchorage.

Inside the Flow itself a call for help is normally answered by whichever station is the nearer. However, most of these missions, described by the Royal National Lifeboat Institution with characteristic understatement merely as 'services', take place round the coast outside - for Stromness, on the exposed iron-hard west side of Orkney; for Longhope, in the confusion of the Pentland Firth's savage, and to the layman, unpredictable tides and weather. And when these 'Mayday' calls come, that weather is often at its very worst; storm-force winds piling up tremendous seas with 60-foot-high waves at times - 'liquid cliffs' they have been called - and the real rocks are never far away. Putting to sea in such conditions, when others are wisely seeking shelter, demands superb seamanship and courage of the highest order. That the men who man the Orkney lifeboats have always had both these qualities in full measure is borne out by their records and by the fact that over the years they have been awarded no fewer than 15 silver and eight bronze medals for gallantry which are appropriately inscribed with the Psalmist's prayer '. . . let not the deep swallow me up.'

A third Orkney lifeboat has been stationed at Kirkwall since 1972 to cover the North Isles and eastern seaboard. For several years before that it had been operating in a cruising role in the North Isles finally being based permanently at Kirkwall. In the comparatively short period of its existence it has rescued over 100 people since taking over from the Stronsay boat which itself saved over 50 lives while operating both before and after the first World War when the herring fishing was at its peak and again for a few years after World War II.

During the 126 years between 1867, when the first Orkney lifeboat came into service, and 1993, boats from these four stations saved close on a thousand lives - 966 in all - and the good work goes on. Even with all the advances in modern science and technology ships can, and still do come to grief putting the lives of those on board at risk.

That first boat was stationed at Stromness, a busy mercantile and fishing port at the time with a constant ebb and flow of shipping. Just the year before, on New Year's Day 1866, an immigrant ship, the *Albion*, had gone ashore on the island of Graemsay just opposite the harbour entrance. Although most of the passengers and crew were saved by an *ad hoc* fleet of local rescue craft one boat overturned and 11 men were lost emphasising what had long been obvious to seafarers and especially to Orcadians through bitter experience - that Orkney with its rock-bound coastline, treacherous tides and often appalling weather was a perilous place for shipping. The Royal National Lifeboat Institution was petitioned to provide a boat specially designed to cope with such emergencies and in October 1867, less than two years later, that boat duly arrived, to be manned, as have all the Stromness and Orkney lifeboats ever since, by local volunteers. It was the beginning of a long, treasured and continuing association between Orkney and the RNLI.

Like all lifeboats of her time, of course, she was powered by sail and oars alone, a far cry from the sophisticated craft of today with their advanced hull-design, powerful engines, radio and electronic navigational aids. But the vital factors in the saving of over 300 lives achieved since then by the boats which have followed in the Stromness station remain the skill and dedication of their crewmen.

Longhope's first lifeboat was in operation seven years later, in 1874, since when a succession of Longhope boats have saved nearly 500 lives in many hazardous services.

In March 1969, however, one of them ended in tragedy. The Longhope boat, *TGB*, answered a call for help from the 3200 ton cargo ship, *Irene*, wallowing helplessly out of control east of South Ronaldsay. A force 9 sou'easterly gale blowing for three days had piled up a vicious pattern of huge waves in the area and in the darkness one of them, even bigger than the rest, overwhelmed *TGB* drowning all eight of her crew including the coxswain, Dan Kirkpatrick, holder of three RNLI silver medals, and two of his sons, Daniel and John, the mechanic, Robert Johnstone, and his two sons, James and Robert, along with Eric McFadyen and James Swanson. It was a devastating blow to such a small community of only a few hundred people.

Having been swept back through the Firth by the

ebb tide, *TGB* with the bodies of seven of her crew was found next day only a few miles off Brims from where she set out on her last ill-fated mission. Jim Swanson's body was never found but he, like the others, is remembered on the memorial in Kirk Hope graveyard unveiled by Queen Elizabeth, the Queen Mother, whose Caithness home, the Castle of Mey, looks out across the Firth to Scapa Flow.

During the period when Longhope was without a boat the Kirkwall lifeboat operating from Scapa Pier covered the Pentland Firth and provided training for the new Longhope crew.

Within 18 months this tiny community had produced another fully-trained volunteer crew with Jack Leslie of the Stromness boat as coxswain and Ian McFadyen, whose brother had been lost in the *TGB*, as mechanic, ready to take their new boat to sea whenever the call came. Such is the spirit of dedication in the Lifeboat Service.

Facts, Figures and Points of View

'The time has come,' the Walrus said,
'To talk of many things:
Of shoes - and ships - and sealing wax -
Of cabbages - and kings.'

LEWIS CARROLL -
The Walrus and the Carpenter

What and Where It Is

The main anchorage of Scapa Flow is an area of some 270 square miles (700 sq km) of open but sheltered water roughly 16 miles by 17 (25 x 27 km) in extent enclosed by the South Isles of Orkney and separated from the north coast of Scotland by the Pentland Firth tideway just over 6 miles (9.5 km) across at its narrowest between Burwick in South Ronaldsay and John o' Groats in Caithness.

It is sheltered by the Orkney Mainland to the north, and eight other islands, Lamb Holm, Glims Holm, Burray and South Ronaldsay to the east, Flotta, Switha and South Walls to the south, Hoy and Graemsay to the west. Hoy with North and South Walls are all parts of the same island.

Originally there were seven narrow entrances to the Flow between these islands, all with strong tides of up to 10 knots (18.2 kph) and none of them wider than three miles (4.8 km) or so across. The main channels used by the Navy were Hoxa and Switha Sounds on either side of Flotta to the south and to a lesser extent, Hoy Sound on the west. Four of these channels, Holm, Skerry, East Weddell and Water Sounds on the eastern approaches were permanently sealed against sea-borne attack during World War II when the islands of South Ronaldsay, Burray, Glims Holm and Lamb Holm, were joined to the Orkney Mainland by the Churchill Barriers. Blockships were also sunk across them in both World Wars so that only the three entrances of Hoxa, Switha and Hoy Sounds are now navigable by ships of any size.

The sea floor of the Flow is generally good level

holding ground with an average depth of 120 feet (36 metres) the lowest point being in the Bring Deeps off Hoy where it goes down to 180 feet (55 m) but there is an even greater depth just outside in Hoxa Sound at 200 feet (61 m).

Within the Flow itself there are a few small islands, all of them now uninhabited, the Calf of Flotta, Cava, Fara and Rysa Little to the north of Flotta, the Holm of Houton off the Mainland shore in Orphir, Hunda off Burray and now joined to it by a causeway, and a skerry, the Barrel of Butter, in the middle, so-called from the rental which once had to be paid for the right to take seals there.

Highest points round the Flow are on Hoy to the west where the Ward Hill rises to 1532 feet (467 m) and to the north, on the Mainland, with the Ward Hill of Orphir at 857 feet (268 m) and Wideford Hill near Kirkwall, 750 feet (225 m). To the east the ground is relatively flat and low-lying.

Distances from Stanger Head on Flotta at the southern main entrance to Scapa Flow are :

John o' Groats (Caithness) 11 miles (18 km)
Duncansby Head 12 miles (19.6 km)
Dunnet Head 14.5 miles (23 km)
Invergordon (mainland naval base) 80 miles (128 km)
Rosyth, (naval base) 230 miles (370 km)
Whitehall, London (Admiralty) 690 miles (1100 km)
Stavanger, Norway 310 miles (496 km)
Bergen, Norway 320 miles (512 km)
Kiel, Germany (naval base) 600 miles (960 km)
Wilhelmshaven, Germany (naval base) 540 miles (860 km)
Jutland Bank, North Sea 400 miles (640 km)
Reykjavik (Iceland) 675 miles (1080 km)

The Orkney group as a whole numbers close on 100 islands, some mere rocks or skerries, contained within an area of about 1750 square miles (4532 sq km) of sea off the north coast of Scotland. With the North Sea on one side and the Atlantic Ocean on the other they stretch northwards from Burwick in South Ronaldsay on the Pentland Firth 46 miles (73km) to Mull Head in Papa Westray and from Start Point in Sanday on the east for 38 miles (61 km) westwards.

With a total population of just over 20,000 at the 1991 census only 17 of the islands had more than two or three people living on them. When World War I broke out in 1914 the native population had dropped, largely through emigration, from its peak of over 32,000 in the 1860s to less than 26,000. At the outbreak of World War II in 1939 Orkney was home for only 22,000 people and even that total had dropped to just on 17,000 in the 1960s before the advent of North Sea oil boosted it to its present level.

For over 5000 years Orkney has enjoyed, or suffered, a continuous ebb and flow of many different peoples, through its islands, Neolithic and Bronze Age men, Picts, Norsemen, Scots, and particularly during the two wars, Englishmen, as well as many others besides, all of whom have left their genetic imprint on the native population. As the Stromness poet and author, George Mackay Brown, has written, we Orcadians are indeed '. . . a fine mixter-maxter.'

"Firsts"

9 July 1915 - First Royal Investiture at Scapa - Vice Admiral Sir Stanley Colville, Vice Admiral Commanding Orkney and Shetland (ACOS) received the Grand Cross of the Victorian Order (GCVO) from George V in the Longhope Hotel (HQ ACOS).

12 Jan 1916 - First depth charge used SE of Pentland Skerries. U-boat damaged.

5 Aug 1917 - First take-off and landing on an aircraft carrier under way. Commander Edwin Dunning in a Sopwith Pup took off from *HMS Furious* steaming at 30 knots in the Flow and landed back again safely on her flight deck. He was killed shortly afterwards when attempting a similar landing.

28 Oct 1918 - *UB 116* blown up and sunk by mines in Hoxa Sound fired from a shore station in Flotta - the first, and only submarine to be destroyed in a controlled minefield in World War I. The submarine was detected on indicator loops when making a last desperate attempt to penetrate the Scapa defences at the end of the war. It was also the last U-boat to be destroyed in that war.

1939 - Hatston *(HMS Sparrowhawk)* one of the first airfields in UK to have tarmac runways.

13/14 Oct 1939- *U 47* (Lieut Cmdr Gunther Prien) became first submarine ever to penetrate the Scapa defences getting in at high water through Kirk Sound on the Mainland side between Holm and Lamb Holm to torpedo and sink the 27,000-ton battleship *Royal Oak* at anchor about a mile off Gaitnip with the loss of 833 lives. *U 47* escaped undamaged through the same channel on the south side.

17 Oct 1939 - Morning - First air raid on Scapa Flow and the first German aircraft (Ju 88) to be shot down on British soil by anti-aircraft gunfire in World War II. Shot down by 226 HAA Bty RA, TA, manned by Orkney and Caithness gunners. Crashed near Pegal Burn in Hoy after dive-bomb attack on *HMS Iron Duke* moored off Lyness. *Iron Duke* was holed and beached.

17 Oct 1939 - Afternoon - Second attack (high level) on the Flow and the first German bomb to explode on British soil in World War II. It fell on Ore Farm near Lyness causing no damage. Luftwaffe had strict orders at this time to attack only targets at sea and not to drop any bombs on land.

16 March 1940 - First British civilian air raid casualty in World War II. John Isbister killed by bombs at Brig o' Waithe in Stenness during dusk raid on ships in the Flow.

2 April 1940 - Anti-aircraft barrage tried out for the first time.

10 April 1940 - 16 Fleet Air Arm single-engined Skua dive bombers of 800 and 803 Squadrons from Hatston led by Captain R.T. Partridge RM attacked and sank the German heavy cruiser, *Konigsberg*, in Bergen harbour, Norway - the first major warship ever to have been sunk by aircraft alone.

25 December 1940 - First enemy aircraft (Ju 88) to be shot down in World War II by an American-built fighter (Grumman Martlet) manned by Royal Navy aircrew. Crash-landed intact on farm near Skeabrae airfield and the crew were taken prisoner by the farmer Capt. T. Harcus who had himself been a prisoner-of-war in the first World War.

1940 - Scapa communications centre first to operate teleprinters over radio link instead of land line.

April 1942 - Hatston (*HMS Sparrowhawk*) was one of the first, if not the first, airfield in Britain to house and train members of the US Navy Air Force after America entered

the war in December 1941. The aircraft carrier *Wasp* came
into the Flow as part of a task force and flew off three
squadrons of Vindicator aircraft to Hatston where their
crews trained and took part in operations for five weeks
before embarking again for the Mediterranean.

3 February 1956 - When the Norwegian ship *Dovrefjell*
went ashore on the Pentland Skerries during a southerly
gale the Longhope and Wick lifeboats were unable to get
near enough to take the crew off. The Flag Officer Scotland
and Northern Ireland was in the Flow on a routine visit
and ordered two naval helicopters from Lossiemouth and
an RAF helicopter from Leuchars to come north. In a
shuttle service they took the 42 crewmen from the wreck to
Caithness in a three-hour operation - the first time
helicopters had been used for a civilian rescue.

Major Disasters

HMS HAMPSHIRE on passage from Scapa Flow to Archangel in Russia with British Secretary for War, Field Marshall Lord Kitchener on board struck mine(s) off Marwick Head in Birsay during NW gale in the evening of 5 June 1916 and sank in less than 15 minutes with only 12 survivors. Kitchener and his staff, on their way to confer with the Czar and Russian military leaders about aid for the Eastern Front, were among those lost. Weather was so bad that the two-destroyer escort had been forced to return to harbour.

Naval authorities clamped down on security refusing to allow the Stromness lifeboat to put to sea and they also prevented local people in the area from going to the shores and cliffs where they would probably have been able to save many lives.

Within days of the disaster a local appeal was launched to provide a memorial to him as a result of which the square tower on Marwick Head was erected and dedicated in 1926.

HMS PHEASANT, newly commissioned M Class destroyer lost with all 102 hands off Hoy on 1 March, 1917. Probably mined.

HMS VANGUARD, a battleship with a ship's company of over 1000 blew up and sank while at anchor with the rest of the Grand Fleet off Flotta in Scapa Flow just before midnight on 9 July 1917. There were only two survivors. It is believed the cause of the internal explosion was the ignition of unstable cordite. With some 1000 men dead this is the worst disaster ever to have occurred in the

Flow. *Vanguard* was the third British warship to blow up while at anchor during World War I - the other two were the battleship *Bulwark* off Sheerness in 1914 and the cruiser *Natal* at Cromarty in 1915.

HMS OPAL and *HMS NARBOROUGH*, two destroyers returning to base in Scapa Flow from a North Sea patrol during a gale with blizzard conditions on the night of 12/13 January 1918 struck Hesta Head on the east side of South Ronaldsay and broke up. There was only one survivor from the two ships.

HMS ROYAL OAK torpedoed and sunk by German submarine *U 47* while at anchor on the north side of Scapa Flow off Gaitnip on the night of 13/14 October 1939 with the loss of 833 men out of her ship's company of about 1400. The U-boat commander, Gunther Prien, in a great feat of daring seamanship managed to find two gaps in the inadequately blocked eastern channel of Kirk Sound. *Royal Oak* was the only capital ship in the anchorage that night the rest of the Fleet, apart from a few destroyers and auxiliaries, having put to sea earlier in the day. The 27,000 ton battleship was hit by three torpedoes and sank in 15 minutes. *U 47* escaped and returned to a hero's welcome in Germany but was subsequently depth-charged and destroyed off Iceland by *HMS Wolverine*. *Royal Oak* still lies less than a mile off shore and is an official war grave.

LONGHOPE LIFEBOAT TGB was lost with all eight of her crew when answering a call for assistance from the Greek-owned 2300 ton cargo ship *Irene* broken down and drifting helpless in a force 9 gale off South Ronaldsay, on the night of 17/18 March 1969. The three-day gale had whipped up waves of 60 feet or more, one of which overwhelmed the lifeboat.

By an irony of fate all 17 of the *Irene*'s crew were safely rescued by breeches buoy after she drifted ashore on South Ronaldsay.

Famous Visitors

*indicates visit was before World War II

Royals

*GEORGE V - July 1898: as Duke of York when commanding cruiser *HMS Crescent* with Channel Fleet anchored in Kirkwall Bay.

17 July 1915: spent several days visiting and inspecting ships of the Grand Fleet and shore establishments including coast defence batteries on Stanger Head, Flotta. Stayed at Base HQ in Longhope Hotel with Admiral Commanding Orkney and Shetland (ACOS) Vice Admiral Sir Stanley Colville. June 1915: spent several days in the Flow aboard *HMS Iron Duke*, Flagship of Admiral Sir John Jellicoe, Commander-in-Chief of the Grand Fleet which a few days before had been in action at the Battle of Jutland. 21 June 1917: last visit to Scapa when he stayed on board *HMS Queen Elizabeth*, Flagship of Admiral Sir David Beatty, then C-in-C, Grand Fleet.

*EDWARD, PRINCE OF WALES (later Edward VIII) - August 1915: spent a week inspecting ships and defences. Stayed at Longhope Hotel with Admiral Colville (ACOS).

*PRINCE GEORGE (later Duke of Kent) - August 1920: in Training Ship *HMS Temeraire*.

GEORGE VI - August 1914: as *Prince Albert, Midshipman in battleship *Collingwood*. Served in Scapa some two years sailing from there to take part in the Battle of Jutland, May 1916.

5 October 1939: arrived in cruiser *Aurora* staying aboard *HMS Nelson*, Flagship of C-in-C Home Fleet,

Admiral Sir Charles Forbes, visiting the Fleet and shore establishments including Fleet Air Arm station at Hatston *(HMS Sparrowhawk)* and Lyness naval base to meet crews of fishing boats requisitioned for patrol work and gunners of 226 HAA Bty, the Orkney and Caithness unit. 9 August 1941: landed by RAF bomber at Hatston before going out to the Fleet in the Flow where he again stayed aboard *Nelson* while inspecting ships and the 2nd Battalion Orkney Home Guard at Lyness. June 1942: again with the Home Fleet in the Flow. March 1943: arrived in destroyer *Milne* and stayed aboard the Flagship visiting ships, Twatt airfield *(HMS Tern)*, and a military hospital. 10 May 1944: visited Fleet just before D-Day, going to sea on an exercise in the aircraft carrier, *Victorious.*

OLAF, Crown Prince (later King) of Norway - October 1941: accompanied by Admiral Reiser Larsen, Officer Commanding Norwegian Air Force visited 331 (all-Norwegian) Hurricane Squadron at Skeabrae.

HAAKON VII of Norway - May 1944: visiting Norwegian ships before D-Day.

GEORGE II of the Hellenes - May 1944.

All three monarchs, George VI, Haakon VII and George II of the Hellenes were in the Flow at the same time.

Other VIPs

ALANBROOKE, Field Marshall Lord - 1939: as Chief of the Imperial General Staff. May 1941: as C-in-C Home Forces.

ALEXANDER, A.V. - Several visits from 1941 as First Lord of the Admiralty. July 1945: opened Churchill Causeways.

*ASQUITH, H.H. - <u>October 1913:</u> as Prime Minister with Winston Churchill, then First Lord of the Admiralty.

CAMPBELL, Very Revd A.J. - <u>1945:</u> Moderator of the General Assembly of the Church of Scotland. Minister of the Evie Church in Orkney.

*CHAMBERLAIN, Neville - <u>August 1939:</u> when Prime Minister flew over Flow while returning to Downing Street from holiday in Scotland just before the outbreak of war.

COCKBURN, Very Revd Dr J. Hutchison - <u>July 1941:</u> Moderator of the General Assembly of the Church of Scotland.

CHURCHILL, Winston Spencer - <u>October 1913:</u> as *First Lord of the Admiralty with Prime Minister Asquith prior to high level naval conference at Cromarty. They visited Kirkwall on foot walking from Scapa Pier into town and back.

<u>16 September 1939:</u> again as First Lord, to assess defence requirements for the Base. Stayed aboard the Flagship *HMS Nelson.* <u>8 March 1940:</u> on board *HMS Hood* for the return of the Home Fleet to its Scapa Base after the build-up of the defences following the first attacks by U-boat and Luftwaffe in <u>October 1939.</u> Final decision taken to build the Churchill Barriers across the eastern channels. <u>February 1941:</u> now Prime Minister, came north to Scapa to see Lord Halifax off aboard *HMS King George V,* to take up his appointment as Britain's ambassador to USA. <u>4 August 1941:</u> arrived Scapa to board *HMS Prince of Wales* on his way to the Atlantic Charter meeting with President Roosevelt returning to Scapa via Iceland <u>18 August 1941.</u>

HALIFAX, Lord - <u>February 1941:</u> left from Flow on his way to take up appointment as ambassador to the USA. (see Churchill).

HOPKINS, Harry - <u>February 1941:</u> President Roosevelt's special envoy he joined Churchill in Scapa to bid farewell to Lord Halifax on his way to USA.

*KITCHENER, Field Marshall Lord - <u>5 June 1916:</u> as

Secretary of State for War boarded the cruiser *Hampshire* for passage to Russia. Lost same day when *Hampshire* was mined off west coast of Orkney.

*LANG, Dr Cosmo - <u>Summer 1915:</u> Archbishop of York (later Archbishop of Canterbury) visited Home Fleet. Dedicated Anglican section of Lyness naval cemetery. First Anglican Archbishop to set foot on Orkney soil.

*MacKENNA. Reginald - <u>1911:</u> as First Lord came to Scapa on a cruise in the Admiralty yacht *Enchantress*.

MONTGOMERY, Field Marshall Lord (Monty) - <u>May 1944:</u> flying pep visit prior to D-Day.

PILE, General Sir Freddie - <u>1941:</u> C-in-C AA Command.

SINCLAIR, Sir Archibald - <u>January 1940</u> on a fact-finding mission to assess defence priorities. Leader of the Liberal Party later to become Air Minister. His home was Thurso Castle just across the Pentland Firth from the Hoxa entrance to the Flow.

*SPENCE, Graeme - <u>prior to 1812</u>: Maritime Surveyor to the Admiralty who first proposed Scapa Flow as a 'Fleet Rendezvous'.

Artistes

Artistes who entertained the troops at Scapa included:

Leslie Henson, Tommy Handley, Vera Lynn, Gracie Fields, George Formby, Flanagan and Allan, Will Hay, Evelyn Laye, Gertrude Lawrence, Francoise Rosay, Beatrice Lillie, Douglas Byng, Tommy Trinder.

Yehudi Menuhin, Pouishnoff, Joan Hammond, Leon Goossens, Boyd Neal Orchestra.

But during World War I the music-hall stars Harry Lauder and Henry Tait were refused permission to entertain servicemen at Scapa on 'security' grounds

Service Chiefs

World War I

Navy

BEATTY, Admiral Sir (later Earl) David - Commanded 1st Battlecruiser Squadron in 1914 subsequently succeeding Jellicoe as C-in-C Grand Fleet in 1916. Received surrender of German High Seas Fleet in the Forth in November 1918.

COLVILLE, Vice Admiral Sir Stanley - Admiral Commanding Orkney and Shetland (ACOS) 1914..

FREMANTLE, Vice Admiral Sir Sydney - Commanded 1st Battle Squadron 1919 in the Flow when interned German fleet was scuttled.

JELLICOE, Admiral Sir (later Viscount) John - C-in-C Grand Fleet July 1914 to November 1916. Sailed from the Flow May 1916 for the Battle of Jutland.

REUTER, Admiral Ludwig von - Commanded interned German High Seas Fleet in the Flow from November 1918 till the scuttle on 21 June 1919.

World War II

Navy

BINNEY, Vice Admiral T.H. - ACOS December 1939.

FORBES, Sir Charles - C-in-C Home Fleet 1939.

FRENCH, Admiral Sir William - ACOS August-December 1939.

HORTON, Vice Admiral Max - commanding Northern Patrol 1939/40.

MOUNTBATTEN, Captain (later Admiral) Lord Louis - Captain (D) commanding 5th Flotilla of K Class destroyers from his flagship *HMS Kelly* while working up in the Flow during November 1939 and took part in the 1940 Norwegian campaign.

WELLS, Vice Admiral L.V. - ACOS January 1942.

Army

KEMP, Brigadier (later Major General) Geoffrey - Commander Orkney and Shetland Defences (OSDeF) September 1939-January 1943.

SLATER, Major General - Commander OSDeF January 1943.

A Matter of Opinion

Writing in Sir John Sinclair's 'Old Statistical Account of Scotland' at the end of the 18th century, the Orphir minister, the Reverend Francis Liddell, whose manse looked out over Scapa Flow described it as '. . . a most beautiful piece of water, being a small Mediterranean about fifty miles in circumference.'

It is very doubtful, however, if many of those who served on its defences in the two World Wars would agree with him. Beautiful? Well, perhaps sometimes, depending on the weather and the eye of the beholder - but the Mediterranean? Emphatically no. And in both wars these soldiers and sailors resorted to verse, of a kind, to describe what they fervently hoped would be no more than a very temporary posting. From World War I came this 'Hymn of Hate '-

Have you ever heard the story of how Scapa got its name?
If you haven't then you're slow because it's earned a world-wide fame,
It has caused a lot of howling amongst our tars at sea,
So I'll tell to you the story as a sailor told it me.

Sure a little bit of wastage fell from out the sky one day,
And it fell into the ocean in a spot up Scotland way.
And when the Sea Lords saw it, sure it looked so bleak and bare
They said 'Suppose we start to build a naval base up there.'

So they dotted it with colliers, to provide the tars with work,
With provision boats and oilers, that they dared not dodge or shirk;
Then they sprinkled it with raindrops, with sleet and hail and snow,
And when they had it finished, sure they called it Scapa Flow.

Now the Navy's been at Scapa ever since we've been at war,
And whenever it is over, they won't want to see it more,
And for years and years to come, whenever sailors congregate,
You can bet your life you'll hear them sing that Scapa Hymn of Hate.

One of their Commanders-in-Chief, Admiral Sir
David Beatty, didn't much care for it either, except
strategically, writing of it in a letter as '. . . this cursed
region where it is blowing a gale of wind and where the
sun never shines.' His predecessor, Admiral Jellicoe, who
built up the Base, while not committing himself as to
Scapa's scenic or climatic splendours or otherwise, except
in his professional capacity as a naval officer, had no
doubts as to its value from that standpoint describing it
succinctly just as 'a fine stretch of water' and adding that
it was '. . . the centre and pivot of the whole naval side of
the war.'

An RNVR Sub Lieutenant who subsequently became
Captain A. R. Williamson, specialising in anti-submarine
netting devices, called in at the Flow for the first time early
in 1915 aboard *HMS Crescent* and noted in his diary – '. . . I
found that Scapa Flow is an inland sea surrounded by the
islands of Hoy and Ronaldsay and other lumps of mud
which appear on the map as part of the Orkney Islands,
and as the straits – 3 in number, 2 being now blocked up
for the exigencies of war – are very narrow and tortuous
the enclosed sheet of water is the most glorious harbour
and an ideal base for the part of the Battle Fleet which is at
present lying here. When day dawned this morning
(January 30) we could see them all lying there in beautiful
array – Dreadnoughts, battle-cruisers, swift light cruisers
and a swarm of torpedo destroyers all wating to rush forth
and tie the German Navy up in every conceivable form of
knot.'

These were some of the navymen's more printable
opinions of Scapa in World War I, views apparently shared

by their erstwhile enemies during the internment there of the German Fleet after the Armistice in 1918. One of them wrote home to a Hamburg newspaper - 'If the English have stood this for four years, they deserve to have won the war.'

A quarter of a century later the soldiers had a go and they were even less complimentary but certainly even more forceful than the sailors, not merely confining their bored antipathy to the Flow itself but extending it to most of the surrounding islands as well in these scathing verses entitled 'Bloody Orkney' in 'The Orkney Blast.'

This bloody town's a bloody cuss,
No bloody trains, no bloody bus,
And no one cares for bloody us,
In bloody Orkney.

The bloody roads are bloody bad,
The bloody folks are bloody mad,
They'd make the brightest bloody sad,
In bloody Orkney.

All bloody clouds and bloody rain,
No bloody kerbs, no bloody drains,
The Council's got no bloody brains,
In bloody Orkney.

Everything's so bloody dear,
A bloody bob for bloody beer,
And is it good? - No bloody fear,
In bloody Orkney.

The bloody flicks are bloody old,
The bloody seats are bloody cold,
You can't get in for bloody gold,
In bloody Orkney.

The bloody dances make you smile,
The bloody band is bloody vile,
It only cramps your bloody style,
In bloody Orkney.

No bloody sport, no bloody games,
No bloody fun, the bloody dames,
Won't even give their bloody names,
In bloody Orkney.

Best bloody place is bloody bed,
With bloody ice on bloody head,
You might as well be bloody dead,
In bloody Orkney.

The despised locals took a poor view of this denigration of their islands and way of life responding vigorously and no less forcibly in 'Hell's Bells' also featured in 'The Orkney Blast' -

The bloody Sassenachs have come,
With bugle call and tuck of drum,
With smell of beer and Army rum,
The cheeky sods.
What right have they to criticise,
Who blow their trumpets to the skies,
But all our folk and homes despise,
The bloody clods.

We love the winds, we like the rains,
We DO have kerbs and likewise drains,
We have no trams or railway trains,
But ships and luggers.
O could we hear the farewell knell,
Of old St Magnus Church's bell,
To send them all to bloody hell,
The cocky buggers.

But not all the servicemen in either war subscribed wholly to the first two splenetic outbursts. Some even found it sufficiently attractive to come back in peacetime for holidays and quite a few to settle round its shores giving those anonymous 'bloody dames' their own 'bloody names' by marrying them.

Perhaps they had seen it as Eric Linklater, the Orcadian author who also served on the defences, described it at the beginning of September 1939 as the last hours of peace ticked away before the 'dogs of war' were finally 'let slip' -

'On calm days the islands floated on a deep-blue sea in a charm of shadowed cliffs and reddish moors, the harvest was ripe, and the fields were bearded with bright gold or gay in a lovely green. The forehead of the hills rose in smooth lines against a lucent sky, and rippled lakes provoked a passion for mere water. In such weather one could live by the eye alone, and beautify oneself with the delighted torture of love-at-seventeen. To suppose that war might invade that landscape, or snatch one from it, seemed quite outrageous; yet it was, beyond doubting the threat of war that opened one's eyes, as if to a new thing, to the beauty of the islands and their sea.'

But knowing Orkney as intimately as he did, he was by no means blind to the other and grimmer face the Flow could present while still finding in it a majestic beauty and a feeling of exhilaration as he did when writing, again in 'The Art of Adventure'-

'To stand in a south-easterly gale on the weather-worn headlands of Hoxa and Stanger, at the Fleet's entrance to Scapa Flow, was to endure such a hurly-burly, so rude and ponderous a buffeting, that one could hardly deny a sense of outrage, a suspicion that the wind's violence was a personal enmity. In the crested tumult of the sea there were colours of wildly derisive beauty above the monstrous procession of the waves, and the spectator, battered by the gale, and resentful, was humbled by the immensity of the pageant that careered before it. The sky was pitiless, and the young soldiers in their shabby khaki were dwarfed and lonely in the vast confusion of the storm.'

This, then, was how various people of all ranks and conditions felt about what Winston Churchill, on his visit to the Flow in 1940 while First Lord of the Admiralty, called 'the great lake of Scapa . . . the famous home from which in the previous war the Royal Navy had ruled the seas' and would do so again in the second war.

Books for Further Reading

Bailey, P. - Orkney
Brown, M. & Meehan, P. - Scapa Flow
Burrows, C.W. - Scapa and a Camera
Cormack, A. & A. - Bolsters, Blocks, Barriers
Fereday, R. P. - Martello Towers
Ferguson, David M. - The Wrecks of Scapa Flow
Hamilton, J.R.E. - Coast Defence of Orkney in Two World Wars
Hewison, W.S. - This Great Harbour - Scapa Flow
Jellicoe, John - The Grand Fleet, 1914-1916
Korgonoff, A. - The Phantom of Scapa Flow
Lamb, Gregor - Sky Over Scapa
Linklater, Eric - The Art of Adventure, Northern Garrisons
Marwick, H. - Orkney
McKee, A. - Black Saturday
Miller, R. - Orkney
Reuter, L. von - Scapa Flow; the Account of the Greatest
    Scuttle of All Time
Roskill, C.S. - The War at Sea, Vol I (Official History)
Royle, T. - The Kitchener Enigma
Ruge, F. - Scapa Flow 1919, the End of the German Fleet
Smith, P.I. - Naval Wrecks of Scapa Flow
Snyder, G.S. - The Royal Oak Disaster
van der Vat, Dan - The Grand Scuttle
Weaver, H.J. - Nightmare at Scapa Flow

Museums

There are several collections of artefacts connected
with Scapa Flow including that in the maritime section of
Stromness Museum which has many items from the
salvaged German Fleet; the Lyness Visitor Centre which
tells visually the Scapa story on the site where much of it
actually happened; the Wireless Museum in St Margaret's
Hope across the Churchill Barriers with interesting
examples of how radio and radar were used in the Scapa
defences; and for an overall view of Orkney through the
ages from Norse times onward and before there is
Tankerness House Museum just opposite St Magnus
Cathedral in Kirkwall.

Index

List of Plates

We are greatly indebted to the following sources for use of photographs:

E.E.C. ..... Elf Enterprise Caledonia.
I.W.M. ... Imperial War Museum
O.C.L. ... Orkney County Library.
O.T.C. ..... Orkney Towage Company.
(R.H.) .... Roddie Hibbert Collection.
R.N.L.I. .. Royal National Lifeboat Institution.
S.M. .... Stromness Museum.
T.H.M. .. Tankerness House Museum.

Cover: Peacetime visit of the Fleet 1911. O.C.L.
1. Martello Tower. T.H.M.
2. Fishing boats at Burray. S.M.
3. Dreadnoughts in Flow. O.C.L.
4. Fleets in Scapa 1909. O.C.L.
5. Flying boat at Houton 1918. T.H.M.
6. Plane overshoots Flight Deck. I.W.M.
7. WWI Battleship *Vanguard*. I.W.M.
8. Navy's Last Battleship, *Vanguard* 1954. I.W.M.
9. RN Submarine and drifter. I.W.M.
10. WWI Blockships in Holm Sound. O.C.L.
11. *HMS Iron Duke*, Flagship at Jutland. S.M.(R.H.)
12. *HMS Nelson*, Flagship Home Fleet 1939. S.M.(R.H.)
13. *HMS Hampshire* 1916. I.W.M.
14. *HMS Royal Oak* at speed. I.W.M.
15. US Navy minesweepers in Kirkwall Bay 1919. O.C.L.
16. A mine explodes. O.C.L.
17. Surrendered German battleship enters Flow 1918. O.C.L.
18. Battleship *Bayern* goes down. S.M.
19. German sailors take to the boats. S.M.
20. *Hindenburg* settled on even keel. S.M.
21. Diver between the wars. S.M.
22. Balloons used to raise destroyer. S.M.
23. Salvaged battleship refloated bottom-up. O.C.L.
24. Salvage work between the wars. S.M.
25. H.M. George V and Admiral Beatty. I.W.M.
26. H.M. George VI enjoys variety show. I.W.M.
27. Bofors LAA gun near Stromness I.W.M.

1. Harvesting beside one of the two Martello Towers, the most northerly in Britain, built during the Napoleonic Wars to guard Longhope - rendezvous harbour for the Baltic convoys.

2. Fishing fleet at Burray - one of the busy herring ports around the Flow which thrived before the wars.

3. Dreadnoughts moored in Scapa Bay before World War I.

4. The Home and Atlantic Fleets of the Royal Navy at anchor in Scapa Flow during the summer cruise of 1909.

5. One of the flying boats based at Houton towards the end of World War I.

6. Commander Edwin Dunning was killed when his Sopwith Pup overshot the flight deck of *HMS Furious* steaming at speed across the Flow in August 1917. Just before this tragic accident he had become the first man ever to succeed in landing an aircraft on a ship under way.

7. The 19,250 ton battleship *Vanguard*, eighth British warship to bear that name, which blew up at anchor in the Flow in July 1917 with the loss of 1000 lives.

8. The ninth *HMS Vanguard*, only completed after World War II and broken up in 1960, was the last British battleship to visit the Flow when she anchored close to where the remains of her namesake still lie on the bottom.

9. A Royal Navy submarine passes one of the patrol drifters in Weddel Sound during World War I.

10. Blockships sunk in Holm Sound during World War I. They were still there in 1939 but were an insufficient obstruction to the U boat which penetrated the defences to sink the *Royal Oak*.

11. *HMS Iron Duke*, Jellicoe's flagship at Jutland in the first war was a Base HQ ship at Lyness in the second when she was holed during the first air attack on the Flow in 1939.

12. *HMS Nelson*, flagship of the Home Fleet in Scapa at the outbreak of War War II.

13. The ill-fated cruiser *Hampshire* sunk by mines off Orkney's west coast in 1916 when Lord Kitchener, Britain's War Minister, on his way to Russia was lost with most of the ship's company.

14 The *Royal Oak* at speed in the Flow with guns cleared for action. She was torpedoed and sunk at anchor off Gaitnip in October 1939 with the loss of 833 lives Now an official war grave she still lies where she sank.

15. Some of the United States minesweepers anchored in Kirkwall Bay while engaged in clearing the North Sea mine barrage during 1919.

16. One of the mines of the North Sea barrage exploding during sweeping operations.

17. The disarmed German battleship *Bayern* creeps through the Hoxa Boom at dawn on 27 November 1919 for internment in the Flow.

18. The *Bayern* takes her final plunge to the bottom when the German Fleet was scuttled on Midsummer Day 1919.

19. German sailors take to the boats in Scapa Flow after opening the seacocks to scuttle their interned destroyer.

20. The scuttled battleship, *Hindenburg*, pride of the Kaiser's navy, which sank on an even keel with her funnels and mast above water was a familiar sight in the Flow between the wars.

21. A diver, in the cumbersome gear needed before scuba diving became commonplace, prepares to go down on one of the sunken German ships.

22. Inflatable balloons were used for flotation in the early attempts to raise some of the smaller German ships.

23. A salvaged German battleship floating bottom up after being raised by compressed air. In order to seal all apertures in the hull while it lay on the seabed salvage men without diving suits gained access from the surface through the airlocks seen projecting above the hulk.

24. Salvage men prepare to go down on one of the scuttled ships.

25. During a visit to the Grand Fleet in Scapa Flow during World War I George V, himself at one time a serving naval officer, chats with the Commander-in Chief, Admiral Sir David Beatty, on the quarterdeck of his flagship the battlecruiser, *Queen Elizabeth*.

26. George VI, who saw action as a naval officer at the battle of Jutland in 1916, relaxes at a troop's variety show during a visit to the Home Fleet in Scapa during World War II.

27. A Bofors Light Anti-Aircraft gun and crew ready for action near Stromness. It could fire 120 two-pound shells a minute.

28. Six-inch coast defence guns in emplacements at Ness Battery near Stromness.

29. Warships in the Flow during the first war towing a kite observation balloon.

30. Swordfish torpedo bombers (Stringbags) on the tarmac at Hatston *(IIMS Spurrowhawk)* with Kirkwall in the background.

31. One of the anti-submarine booms with a boomboat in attendance.

32. German U boat in the Pentland Firth on her way to surrender in Scapa Flow after VE Day.

33. Blockships sunk across the eastern channels in World War II.

34. One of the Churchill Barriers under construction with the blockships it replaced alongside.

35. The road to the isles along the top of the Churchill Barriers was soon in use by civilian transport.

36. The ubiquitous Nissen huts provided accommodation for troops all round the Flow but the Italian prisoners-of-war on Lamb Holm converted this one into a chapel and a work of art in its own right.

37. Flotta oil terminal from the air with the Pentland Firth, Switha Sound and Longhope in the background.

38. Orkney Islands Council tugs in attendance on a tanker at the Single Point Moorings off the Flotta Oil Terminal.

39. The figure of a crewman in full gear by the North Ronaldsay sculptor, Ian Scott, on the memorial in Kirkhope Cemetery to the men who lost their lives in the Longhope Lifeboat disaster.

GREATER LOVE HATH NO MAN THAN THIS, THAT HE LAY DOWN HIS LIFE FOR HIS FELLOWMEN

40. The Longhope lifeboat, *TGB*, lost with all hands when overwhelmed by huge seas while answering a call for help from a broken-down cargo ship drifting helpless in a Force 9 gale off South Ronaldsay on the night of 17/18 March 1969.